EVERYDAY MAGICIANS

THE MAGIC in HISTORY

SOURCEBOOKS SERIES

THE ARRAS WITCH TREATISES
Andrew Colin Gow, Robert B. Desjardins, and François V. Pageau

HAZARDS OF THE DARK ARTS:
ADVICE FOR MEDIEVAL PRINCES ON WITCHCRAFT AND MAGIC
Richard Kieckhefer

ORIGINS OF THE WITCHES' SABBATH
Michael D. Bailey

THE MAGIC OF ROGUES:
NECROMANCERS AND AUTHORITY IN EARLY TUDOR ENGLAND
Frank Klaassen and Sharon Hubbs Wright

The Magic in History Sourcebooks series features compilations and translations of key primary texts that illuminate specific aspects of the history of magic and the occult from within. Each title is tightly focused, but the scope of the series is chronologically and geographically broad, ranging from ancient to modern and with a global reach. Selections are in readable and reliable English, annotated where necessary, with brief contextualizing introductions.

SERIES EDITORS
RICHARD KIECKHEFER
Northwestern University
CLAIRE FANGER
Rice University

EVERYDAY MAGICIANS

LEGAL RECORDS AND MAGIC MANUSCRIPTS

FROM TUDOR ENGLAND

SHARON HUBBS WRIGHT AND FRANK KLAASSEN

The Pennsylvania State University Press

University Park, Pennsylvania

Library of Congress Cataloging-in-Publication Data

Names: Wright, Sharon Hubbs, 1963– author. | Klaassen, Frank F., author.
Title: Everyday magicians : legal records and magic manuscripts from Tudor England / Sharon Hubbs Wright and Frank Klaassen.
Other titles: Magic in history sourcebooks series.
Description: University Park, Pennsylvania : The Pennsylvania State University Press, [2022] | Series: The magic in history sourcebooks series | Includes bibliographical references and index.
Summary: "Examines legal documents and magic texts relevant to common forms of magic practiced in Tudor England"—Provided by publisher.
Identifiers: LCCN 2022021896 | ISBN 9780271093932 (paperback)
Subjects: LCSH: Magic—England—History—16th century—Sources. | Magicians—England—History—16th century—Sources.
Classification: LCC BF1622.E5 W75 2022 | DDC 133.4/30942—dc23/eng/20220711
LC record available at https://lccn.loc.gov/2022021896

Published by The Pennsylvania State University Press,
University Park, PA 16802–1003

The Pennsylvania State University Press is a member of the Association of University Presses.

It is the policy of The Pennsylvania State University Press to use acid-free paper. Publications on uncoated stock satisfy the minimum requirements of American National Standard for Information Sciences—Permanence of Paper for Printed Library Material, ansi z39.48–1992.

FOR JESS, ISAAC, AND AHREN

CONTENTS

ACKNOWLEDGMENTS

Much more than monographs, books of this kind demand the expertise of a wide group of people who deserve our thanks, only the most notable of whom we can thank here. Some of the magic texts presented here began as transcription projects for students in Classical, Medieval, and Renaissance Studies and History at the University of Saskatchewan. Their enthusiasm for uncovering the past has been a source of constant inspiration for us. We thank the staff at the National Archives of Britain, the British Library, the Bodleian Library, the London Metropolitan Archives, and the Borthwick Institute for their wisdom and patience. The work of Owen Davies and Alec Ryre has been particularly valuable in this project and the debt to them will be evident in these pages. We wish to thank Ross Turnbull, Jennifer Hazel, Maud MacInerney, Lauren Kassell, Darrel Rutkin, the two anonymous reviewers, and most particularly, Claire Fanger, Michael Klaassen, and Shannon McSheffrey for lending their expertise to the project. Finally, we thank John Morris (copyeditor) and Elena Gwynne (indexer).

This volume was in part made possible by financial support from the Social Sciences and Humanities Research Council of Canada.

Introduction

The subject of this book is everyday Tudor magicians, both professional and occasional, their activities, and their encounters with authority. The term "everyday" has several senses: performing magic that a significant number of other people also performed or that appears frequently in the written records, being a magician of unexceptional or ordinary quality, being a magician that responded to common concerns, and finally, being perceived by the authorities as a common magician and/or prosecuted in lower courts. All of these qualities have informed the choice of materials presented here. Forms of magic surrounding theft and sickness were very common in Tudor England; they are also very common in manuscripts. Magic focused on love and sex, protection from misfortune, influencing social superiors, winning in games of chance, and getting more money is less frequent in court records but quite frequent in magic manuscripts. In legal terms, most of the magic in this volume was a petty crime, the sort that appeared in the lower courts and most often church courts. The magicians described here were for the most part common folk, and their magic was of a relatively low order in comparison to the high intellectual magic of someone like John Dee or even the Mixindale treasure hunters.[1]

At the same time, the term "everyday magicians" is an approximation, and not all these qualities we have described apply uniformly in every case. Some of the magicians in this volume appear in legal records under suspicion of treason, which was hardly an everyday

---

1. On John Dee, see Deborah E. Harkness, *John Dee's Conversations with Angels: Cabala, Alchemy, and the End of Nature* (Cambridge: Cambridge University Press, 1999); G. J. R. Parry, *The Arch-Conjuror of England: John Dee* (New Haven: Yale University Press, 2011); Benjamin Woolley, *The Queen's Conjurer: The Science and Magic* of Dr. John Dee, Adviser to Queen Elizabeth I (New York: Henry Holt, 2001). On the Mixindale Fellowship, see Frank Klaassen and Sharon Wright, *The Magic of Rogues: Necromancy and Authority in Early Tudor England* (University Park: Penn State University Press, 2021), 83–116.

crime. Some had ambitions to be magicians of a higher order, and the scribes of some of the magic manuscripts seem fairly learned. Some forms of magic that our magicians performed appear frequently in manuscript but infrequently in the courts, and vice versa; we have included a few cases that appear rarely in both manuscript and the court records but speak to mundane concerns and reveal the practices of magic that went on without attracting much notice. Many magicians evidently peddled their wares in the streets and were not hard to find, but we do well to remember that such professionals or semiprofessionals represented no more than 0.03 percent of the population, and probably less.[2]

Most significantly, everyday magic implies a set of practices situated in the everyday world. The comparative analysis of legal and manuscript records, which forms the backbone of this volume, provides an unusually rich field to explore the social aspects of magic practice, and the principal arguments we make in the following pages are focused in this area. First, the most significant identifiable factor that brought a magician to the attention of the authorities was social disruption rather than magic. Second, in comparison to other crimes, it was rare for authorities to prosecute practicing magicians, and the resulting penalties tended to be corporal punishment and/or public penance. In part, as Owen Davies has argued, this was due to a general respect for cunning folk among the populace, but also because authorities had far more pressing problems. Third, magic served key roles in a larger social system. It is uncontroversial that magic helped people cope with particular anxieties. But just as significantly, as in the case of magic surrounding theft, it also filled certain social vacuums in the control of misbehavior that the legal system did not provide. Fourth, although magic was increasingly thought of as a female activity starting in the fifteenth century, it is less clear whether magic practitioners were more commonly male or female, and on balance the numbers were probably more or less equal.[3] Finally, this volume

2. Owen Davies, *Cunning-Folk: Popular Magic in English History* (London: Hambledon & London, 2003), 67–68.

3. Michael D. Bailey, "The Feminization of Magic and the Emerging Idea of the Female Witch in the Late Middle Ages," *Essays in Medieval Studies* 19 (2002): 120–34.

insists that magic practice needs to be separated from the witch trials in order to be properly understood, a subject to which we now turn.

CONTEXT

This book does not concern witches; that is to say, it concerns real magic practitioners. Occasionally magicians were referred to as *sortilegi/-ae* (commonly, but not entirely accurately, translated as witches) or the practices of magicians as witchcraft, so the two categories were not fully distinct. But in all important respects the division between them is critical and stark. The overwhelming majority of people presented in court for witchcraft during the witch trials were not magic practitioners at all, certainly not professional ones. By contrast, most real practitioners never fell afoul of the ecclesiastical or secular authorities, and when they did, it was usually for reasons other than their magic per se. Finally, for most premodern people, witches and cunning folk (i.e., the real magicians they could employ for various purposes) were categorically different kinds of people, not least because cunning folk might protect them from witches. Despite this fact, only in the last few decades has the study of common practitioners begun to be separated from scholarship on witchcraft.[4]

This distinction is important not only for understanding magic practice in the early modern period but also for understanding witchcraft. As Martin Ingram and Eric Midelfort have suggested, one of the failures of witchcraft scholarship has been its lack of attention to the large areas in Europe where there were few witch trials or none at all.[5] This is particularly critical in England, where witch trials were highly localized, resulted in quite low numbers of executions, and, taking into account the whole country and the whole period of the witch trials,

4. See in particular, Davies, *Cunning-Folk.* For a recent study that collapses cunning folk under the heading of witchcraft, see P. G. Maxwell-Stuart, *The British Witch: The Biography* (Stroud, UK: Amberley, 2014).

5. H. C. Erik Midelfort, "Witch Craze? Beyond the Legends of Panic," *Magic, Ritual, and Witchcraft* 6 (2011): 11–33; Martin Ingram, *Church Courts, Sex, and Marriage in England, 1570–1640*, Past and Present Publications (Cambridge: Cambridge University Press, 1987), 96–97.

were more the exception than the rule. In fairness to historians of witchcraft, it is difficult (and much less interesting) to study the *absence* of a thing. However, it is certainly possible to examine the records of real magic practices and practitioners as a point of comparison to the records of the largely imaginary practices of witches.[6] As a result, we have intentionally avoided foregrounding cases from Essex, the main hotbed of witch trials in sixteenth-century England. Knowing what real magic looked like, who practiced it, why some magicians attracted the attention of English authorities, and why others did not is thus a fundamental point of comparison and a key intention of this book.

Common magic practitioners who worked for a fee were referred to as "cunning folk" and the skill they offered as "cunning." The category probably captures many of the magic practitioners in this volume, but it is hard to be sure since many of the cases treat a single incident of magic practice and it is impossible to know if we are seeing a professional or more casual practitioner. Some might also be described as "charmers," although we have not seen strong evidence that this was a clear distinction in the Tudor period.[7] Certainly charms were the most common form of magic and, as Eamon Duffy has demonstrated, employed by all regardless of class and level of education.[8] Nonetheless, the nature of cunning folk and how they were regarded by their society is a good index to understanding everyday magicians.

As Owen Davies has demonstrated, cunning was powerfully associated with literacy and learning.[9] The term was positively inflected and implied respectability, a quality cunning folk needed in order to attract clients. As we shall see in Text 4.1, one was described as "both wise and wealthy, not in a threadbare coat as these imperfect multipliers [i.e., alchemists] commonly are, but well appareled like a cunning man in his craft." Not everyone was happy with what cunning

---

6. Such comparative analysis has been present in the witchcraft literature. See, for example, Alan Macfarlane and J. A. Sharpe, *Witchcraft in Tudor and Stuart England: A Regional and Comparative Study*, 2nd ed. (London: Routledge, 1999).

7. Davies argues the two categories were distinct, but his evidence for this appears to be more modern. Davies, *Cunning-Folk*, 83–84.

8. Eamon Duffy, *The Stripping of the Altars: Traditional Religion in England, 1400–1580*, 2nd ed. (New Haven: Yale University Press, 2005).

9. Davies, *Cunning-Folk*, 71–72.

folk did, nor did everyone believe their magic was efficacious. But the services they offered were generally understood to be positive rather than malefic: healing, identification of thieves or witches, finding lost goods, treasure hunting, and magic for gambling or matters of love. Manuscripts of magic, sometimes no doubt written by cunning folk, quite often reflect these goals and rarely contain malefic operations.

Popular modern accounts often elide premodern cunning folk with witches and tend to represent the local magic practitioner as a "wise woman" who was recondite, was single, and had a dubious reputation due to her mysterious power, which was presumed to be illicit and pagan. None of these ideas correspond well to the historical realities. First, if their magic was not commonly performed in public spaces, cunning folk were certainly public figures. People found out about them from friends and acquaintances who could vouch for them. Their *good* reputation was thus very important, and they sometimes even had testimonial letters from respectable clients (see Text 3.5). Second, most of the powers they claimed to draw upon were not alien. Astrology, astrological influences, and the occult powers of natural objects were conventional ideas in medieval science and parts of medical practice. Many, including female practitioners, used quite conventional medical treatments. Otherwise, the power of their magic lay in the power of Christian religion, despite occasional shreds of pre-Christian ideas or practices.[10] Third, there is no evidence that women were the primary magic practitioners. Davies suggests that cunning folk were significantly more likely to be male in the Tudor period, but the numbers of presentments for magic practice in general (that is, including those who might be nonprofessionals) do not give a clear picture.[11] Women appear more likely to have been accused of magic, particularly in the lower courts.[12] Yet, as the witch trials demonstrate, this cannot be taken as evidence for real practice. On the other hand, the apparently high number of male practitioners may also be illusory. Women's appearances in court records tend to

10. See discussion of Text 5.4 below, p. 104.

11. Davies, *Cunning-Folk*, 68–69.

12. Karen Jones and Michael Zell, "'The Divels Speciall Instruments': Women and Witchcraft Before the 'Great Witch-Hunt,'" *Social History* 30, no. 1 (2005): 45–63.

be recorded with fewer if any descriptive details. The result is that a significant number of the women accused might actually have been practitioners, but this fact is now invisible. Modern historians have also mistaken some female practitioners for men.[13] On balance, our best working assumption is that the numbers of male and female magic practitioners were more or less equal. Lastly, cunning folk were generally understood as the *opposite* of witches and were sometimes employed to protect against witches (see Texts 5.7 and 5.10).[14] By comparison, imputed witches were understood to be disreputable, private and secretive, often poor and illiterate, and more frequently than not female. They had evil intents and acted on private grudges in cooperation with the devil.[15]

What common people thought about magic and its practitioners is not only an important element in understanding premodern magic; it also affected what cases might appear in the courts. Medieval and early modern legal systems relied on individual reports and complaints far more than surveillance by officials. Even in *ex officio* prosecutions in ecclesiastical courts (i.e., cases where a church official presented the case) the action was frequently prompted by rumors. The positive view that most people had of cunning folk and the respectable stratum of society from which they typically came (craftsmen, tradesmen, or farmers) were two of the principal reasons that so few practitioners found themselves in trouble with the authorities.[16] At the same time, the attitude of secular and ecclesiastical authorities toward magic practitioners was ostensibly quite negative and tended to collapse all forms of magic, high and low, imagined and real, into a single category.

13. Hale mistakenly represents Nazareth Jarbrey (Text 2.3) as a man. William Hale, ed., *A Series of Precedents and Proceedings in Criminal Causes Extending from the Year 1475 to 1640: Extracted from Act-Books of Ecclesiastical Courts in the Diocese of London* (London: F. & J. Rivington, 1847), 10–11.

14. James Sharpe, *Witchcraft in Early Modern England* (Harlow, UK: Longman, 2001), 55–56.

15. In Kent in 1396–1543 there were fifteen cases of harmful magic, all of them associated with women. Jones and Zell, "'Divels Speciall Instruments.'"

16. On low levels of accusations against cunning folk and their social status, see Davies, *Cunning-Folk*, 12, 69, and 74–77.

So to understand the whole picture we need to look more closely at the legal bodies that prosecuted magicians.

Ecclesiastical authorities in the sixteenth century had a profoundly negative view of magic and made a good deal of noise about it. In the later Middle Ages, canon law became relatively sophisticated in its knowledge and proscription of magic, particularly learned magic. However, the principal organ of the church's campaign against magic tended to be the pulpit rather than law, and antimagic materials are well represented in late medieval pastoral and proscriptive literature.[17] After the Reformation, attitudes toward magic shifted somewhat, as Protestant invective sometimes elided superstition and magic with Catholicism, but magic continued to receive independent negative attention. For example, a midcentury canon written by reforming bishops called for the gravest penalties (*poenas gravissimas*) for a widely defined set of magical practices, including illicit prayers.[18] It was the expectation of the Church of England that, in regular visitations of their territories, its bishops would seek out and correct "any that vse chames, sorcery, enchauntementes, witchecrafte, southsaying, or any other lyke crafte inuented by the deuyll."[19] This call was repeated in numerous visitation articles published by bishops.[20] However, these texts identified a great number of other sins that needed to be combated as well, and calls for the correction of superstition are commonly buried among scores of other far more pressing sins.

When ecclesiastical authorities got down to the hard business of regulating the behavior of the faithful, magic was a minor, or at least uncommon, issue. Very small numbers of people were presented for

17. See Catherine Rider, *Magic and Religion in Medieval England* (London: Reaktion, 2012).

18. *Reformatio Legum Ecclesiasticarum, Ex Authoritate Primum Regis Henrici. 8. Inchoata: Deinde Per Regem Edouardum 6* (London, 1641), 33. Cited in Francis Young, *Magic as a Political Crime in Early Modern England* (London: Taurus, 2018), 79–80.

19. England and Wales, Sovereign (1509–1547: Henry VIII), *Articles to Be Enquyred of, in the Kynges Maiesties Visitacion* ([London?]: Richardus Grafton regis impressor excudebat, [1547?]), b.i. verso.

20. See, for example, Church of England, Province of Canterbury, Archbishop (1576–1583: Grindal), *Articles to Be Enquired of, within the Prouince of Canterburie, in the Metropoliticall Visitation of the Most Reuerende Father in God, Edmonde Archbishop of Canterburie* (London: [H. Denham for] Willyam Seres, 1576), C.j verso.

magic offenses in visitations or other ecclesiastical processes. In the hundreds of cases (most of which were *ex officio*) in the deanery of Wisbech 1469–1472, only three presentments concerned magic. One person was compurgated, one was fined, and one did public penance.[21] In the 1586 episcopal visitation in Wiltshire, only 7 of 686 presentments (barely 1 percent) were for witchcraft or sorcery, in comparison to 113 for bastardy and illicit pregnancy and 62 for other sexual immorality.[22] Ralph Houlbrooke identifies 1,331 presentments by the Commissary in the archdeaconry of Norwich in 1532–33, 1538–39, and 1549–50. None relate to magic.[23] Of the 1,427 presentments in the visitation of Bishop Still in 1594 in Somerset, only 8 concerned witchcraft. Of these, only 1 was handed over to the local justice of the peace. Only 3 were actually charged and subjected to public penance.[24] In Kent between 1396 and 1543, records suggest that on average slightly more than two people per year were accused either of cursing or magic practice, which are quite distinct and should not be elided (the former not really being magic as such).[25] So, comparatively speaking, magic took up a tiny fraction of the ecclesiastical courts' business. At the same time, the low numbers do not suggest a lack of desire to extirpate magic. Instead, it seems that churchmen had their hands full dealing with other more pressing matters, including the complex fallout of the Reformation.[26]

Secular authorities were similarly vociferous about the need to extirpate magic but were arguably a good deal less effective at doing so. In 1542, Henry's so-called Witchcraft Act attacked conjuring or invocation of spirits, sorceries, and witchcraft. Perhaps predictably, it

21. Lawrence R. Poos, *Lower Ecclesiastical Jurisdiction in Late-Medieval England: The Courts of the Dean and Chapter of Lincoln, 1336–1349, and the Deanery of Wisbech, 1485–1484* (Oxford: Oxford University Press, 2001), 553, 463, and 352–53.

22. Ingram, *Church Courts, Sex, and Marriage*, 68.

23. Ralph A. Houlbrooke, *Church Courts and the People During the English Reformation, 1520–1570*, Oxford Historical Monographs (Oxford: Oxford University Press, 1979), 278–81.

24. Derek Martyn Marsh Shorrocks, *Bishop Still's Visitation 1594: And the "Smale Booke" of the Clerk of the Peace for Somerset, 1593–5* (Taunton, UK: Somerset Record Society, 1998), 18–19, 25, and 142.

25. Jones and Zell, "'Divels Speciall Instruments.'"

26. Houlbrooke, *Church Courts and the People*, 37–38 and 15. See also Jones and Zell, "'Divels Speciall Instruments,'" 58.

elides malefic magic with the more positively intentioned practices of real cunning folk. But it gives much more attention to cunning folk and learned magicians, focusing mostly on treasure hunting, thief identification, finding stolen or lost goods, and love magic. The equipment it mentions, such as "crowns, sceptres, swords, rings, glasses," similarly indicates its main target to be learned practitioners. In the end, however, it had no more than symbolic value, as it was never employed. It may be that suddenly making these activities capital offenses was too draconian for the justices. It may also have been that the habit of regarding magic as a matter for the church courts persisted. One way or another, it was revoked a few years later under Edward VI.

Elizabeth's 1563 Act made a critical distinction between *maleficium* and magic practice. Those convicted of killing others through magic were to be executed, while harming through magic could be subject to lesser punishments. Most practitioners were only subject to temporary imprisonment and pillory, essentially the same punishments the church had imposed in the past. The Act was strengthened under James I and remained in place until it was repealed in 1735. As we shall see, it probably did very little to control real magic practice. Instead, it was employed in the sporadic and localized witch hunts, which swept up quite a different group of people: those who were accused of *maleficium* or bewitchment.

Essex was a hotbed for witchcraft accusations between 1560 and 1700, when we find 299 people indicted there for various magic offenses. This was three times the number of people indicted in Kent in the same period and as much as twelve times the number in Sussex. So Essex was very much the exception to the rule. Nonetheless, it is comparatively well studied and so provides a basis for examining how the 1563 Act was used. Of the 299 people indicted in Essex Assizes 1560–1675 only 9, or roughly 3 percent, were clearly magic practitioners themselves, professional or otherwise. Others were presented for bewitchment or *maleficium*. For the period 1560–1600 alone the percentage of real magic practitioners is a little higher, approximately 6.6 percent (6 cases, or 1 every 6.7 years).[27] More indictments for

27. Alan Macfarlane, *Witchcraft in Tudor and Stuart England: A Regional and Comparative Study* (London: Routledge & Kegan Paul, 1970), 254–303.

magic practitioners appear in the Essex Quarter Sessions between 1565 and 1600, where 5 percent (3 of 58 people identified) were clearly real practitioners, that is, 1 indictment every 12 years.

It must be emphasized that these numbers are based on the data supplied by Macfarlane and in Ewan's abstracts of the cases rather than a thorough reading of the Assize and Quarter Session records. Nonetheless, they give a useful impression of the impact of Elizabeth's legislation on magic practitioners. Given that magic was not against the law prior to 1563 (except 1442–47), these cases by definition represent an increase in the number of indictments for magic practice in the secular courts. At the same time, very few real magic practitioners were caught up in these trials.[28] The legislation and the campaign against witchcraft might well have encouraged practitioners to be more careful, but certainly the overwhelming majority of those implicated under the 1563 Act were innocent of practicing magic.

The cases of Robert Allen, William Neville, and Gregory Wisdom presented below do not derive from indictments for magic per se. At the time of Allen's arrest (and as he himself complained), magic was not against the law. It was his prediction of the death of Edward VI that was at issue. William Neville and Gregory Wisdom were arrested when the 1542 Act was still in effect, but theirs was primarily a case of treason due to plotting the death of a peer of the realm. Despite clear use of magic, they were all released after spending some time in jail. If the authorities were as concerned with practicing magicians as the Acts of 1542 and 1563 suggest, one certainly might expect graver consequences. Even after the 1563 Act was in place, John Prestall, who was patently guilty of magical treason, escaped justice and was able to return to England after a short period of exile.[29] Most practitioners, like John Dee, Simon Forman, and Richard Napier, remained largely or entirely unmolested. It is worth observing that the cunning men like Robert Allen (Text 1.1) were quite aware of the laws that governed the practice of magic, although it is not clear this had any impact on their

28. It is not clear from the evidence presented by Macfarlane if any were executed. A few were found guilty, and some were pilloried.

29. On Prestall, see Michael Devine, "John Prestall: A Complex Relationship with the Elizabethan Regime" (MA thesis, Victoria University of Wellington, 2010); Young, *Magic as a Political Crime*, 91–145.

activities.[30] In short, the secular legislation did very little to control real practitioners.

Presentments in ecclesiastical courts are scattered, but more numerous than those found in secular courts. With the exception of Robert Allen (chapter 1) and Gregory Wisdom (Text 4.1), all the legal documents in this volume are ecclesiastical. Once again, examples from Essex provide an interesting benchmark. Seven people were presented as cunning folk (rather than witches) in the archdeaconry of Essex between 1566 and 1612. This represents less than 6 percent of the cases involving witchcraft and magic, or one every eight years. One notable development is the appearance of a considerable number of presentments for *using the services* of cunning folk. These represent about 16 percent of the presentments concerning magic and witchcraft. Presentments in the archdeaconry of Colchester 1573–1588 are similar. Roughly 8 percent concern actual practitioners, and 5 percent concern those who used their services.

Punishments for magic practice varied widely. In secular courts they ranged from pardons to temporary incarceration to corporal punishment. Thomas Heather of Hoddesen was found guilty of necromantic treasure hunting in 1572 but was pardoned.[31] Robert Browning of Aldham was found guilty of defrauding the king's subjects by persuading them they could get treasure by necromancy in 1598. Like Thomas Fansome (Text 3.5), he was pilloried.[32] There is no known sixteenth-century case of execution of a real magic practitioner for magic alone. In part this probably resulted from the fact that Elizabeth's legislation required only imprisonment and pillory for nonmalefic magic. Those presented and found guilty in ecclesiastical courts were required to do penance, and sometimes this included time in the pillory and/or corporal punishment such as flogging.[33] These courts' goal, as courts

---

30. Stafford, the man who acted as intermediary and brought the magician Gregory Wisdom to Harry Neville, was also aware of the law (Text 4.1).

31. C. L'Estrange Ewen, *Witch Hunting and Witch Trials: The Indictments for Witchcraft from the Records of 1373 Assizes Held for the Home Circuit, A.D. 1559–1736* (London: Kegan Paul, Trench, Trubner, 1929), Case 66 (p. 128). See a partial transcription and translation of the case, 80–81.

32. Ibid., Case 417 (p. 186).

33. See, for example, the public penance and flogging meted out upon nine men, including the ex-mayor of York. Klaassen and Wright, *Magic of Rogues*, 83–116.

of conscience, was, in principle, correction rather than punishment. Nonetheless, the brutality and impact of such punishments should not be understated. It was also well within the power of the church courts to refer a case to the secular courts, where the punishments could be considerably worse.

A critical element in evaluating the records from this period (alluded to above) deserves independent discussion. Cases against women and men do not appear to have been recorded in the same fashion. In Jones and Zell's analysis of court records in Kent, they report that 40 percent of the accusations against women from 1396 to 1543 include no details at all about the offense. This was the case with only 20 percent of men in the same period. After 1543 this number drops to 0 percent for men (i.e., all cases contain details) but remains exactly the same for women.[34] The greater level of attention given to cases concerning men is also very much visible in the records presented in this volume. Although Jones and Zell do not comment on this fact, it is clearly a dramatic and significant difference that must be factored into any effort to understand magic as a gendered activity, or to compare the magical practices of men versus women.

Three things may explain this significant discrepancy in recording. First, Jones and Zell suggest that women were more likely to be accused of malefic magic, and a significant portion of these accusations may genuinely have been based on no substantial evidence. Second, it is possible that there was more concern to establish clear justification in cases against men. Third, women's magic may simply have been regarded as less powerful or less threatening to the social order. Naturally, the last explanation is less plausible in the period of the witch trials, when magic practiced by women was clearly regarded as potentially powerful. Whatever may lie behind the poor record keeping in cases of female magic, the difference must be taken into account when evaluating the surviving records. In comparison to her male counterpart, the female magic practitioner remains a shadowy figure.

34. Jones and Zell, "'Divels Speciall Instruments,'" 53 and 61.

THE MANUSCRIPTS OF MAGIC

Scores of magic manuscripts from sixteenth-century England survive in modern collections. These make clear that significant numbers of people copied, collected, and perhaps practiced this magic. The survival of the manuscripts suggests they did so without interference. The magic they collected was almost uniformly medieval in origin, although sometimes it was adapted to conform to Protestant ideas. Occasionally scribes do evince an awareness of the high magic of the Renaissance, which sought a more expansive and sophisticated incorporation of ancient Hebrew, Neoplatonic, and other traditions.[35] However, books by Ficino, Agrippa, and Pico were expensive, tended toward abstraction, and were written in sophisticated Latin. With very few exceptions, sixteenth-century magicians preferred the practical magic of the Middle Ages that circulated in manuscripts written in more accessible Latin or even English. These texts did not burden the reader with theory but told them what the purpose of an operation was and provided a script for doing it.

These scripts tended to be focused on particular goals, for the most part not that different from the practices of cunning folk: healing, protection, discovering information (particularly the location of treasure, thieves, and stolen goods), and currying love or favor, in addition to a few others such as acquiring learning or creating marvels and illusions. Also, like cunning folk, the scribes of magic manuscripts seem to have steered clear of malefic magic. They did not tend to copy malefic operations unless they were buried in a larger text (e.g., one possible use of a magical image among many). They did, however, record rituals that attacked witches and thieves, which the writers and most other contemporaries no doubt regarded as entirely just. Only magic for love or influence, both of which are relatively common in manuscript, might be considered a form of magical assault, a subject we take up in the introduction to chapter 3.

35. For a cunning man discussing Agrippa, see Klaassen and Wright, *Magic of Rogues*, 43. On medieval versus Renaissance magic, see Frank Klaassen, *Making Magic in Elizabethan England* (University Park: Penn State University Press, 2019), 6–8 and 73–81.

Much of the medieval literature had roots in Hebrew and Arabic traditions and had been developed and transmitted among the learned or clerical elite in the Middle Ages. In the fifteenth and sixteenth centuries, due to rising literacy rates and printing, this literature began to be transmitted to, and translated for, broader audiences. Such was the case with books of secrets or experiments, various forms of astrological magic, and also ritual magic, particularly the invocation of spirits, all of which appear in some form in this volume. As this literature passed into the vernacular languages it was often simplified, adjusted for its new secular environment, creatively reimagined, and sometimes misunderstood or mistranslated. This is also the case with the necromantic (i.e., spirit-conjuring) pieces in this volume. Most medieval necromantic texts were fairly substantial, with most rituals running to several pages and sometimes a dozen or more. The conjurations in this volume are abbreviated versions of such rituals but work on the same principles. They assume that if one used the correct rituals, spirits could be commanded by ritually purified (or at least good) Christians through the power of God. Such invocations also were considerably more likely to succeed under the correct astrological and atmospheric conditions.[36] This literature is closely related to exorcism, which similarly commands evil spirits through divine power. In the Middle Ages, such magic was typically performed by clerics, but it was increasingly transmitted to lay practitioners in the Tudor period.[37]

Charms similarly invoke divine power to cast out evil, in the form of an illness or other misfortune, or to defend the subject from it. In comparison to spirit conjuring, which was a more specialized literature, charms circulated widely and were used by people in all walks of life.[38] They employed simple verbal formulae (sometimes

36. For examples of necromantic practice in sixteenth-century England, see Klaassen, *Making Magic*, 73–135; Klaassen and Wright, *Magic of Rogues*.

37. Richard Kieckhefer, *Magic in the Middle Ages*, Cambridge Medieval Textbooks (Cambridge: Cambridge University Press, 1989), 151–56. For other examples of transmission of learned magic to lay practitioners, see Klaassen and Wright, *Magic of Rogues*, 5.

38. On charms, see Lea Olsan, "Latin Charms of Medieval England: Verbal Healing in a Christian Oral Tradition," *Oral Tradition* 7 (1992): 116–42; Olsan, "The Corpus of Charms in the Middle English Leechcraft Remedy Books," in *Charms, Charmers and Charming: International Research on Verbal Magic*, ed. Jonathan Roper (New York: Palgrave Macmillan, 2009), 214–37. See also Duffy, *Stripping of the Altars*, 266–98.

rhymed), *historiolae* (i.e., short religious stories), conventional prayers, divine names or words of power, and invocations of divine power, often of the saints. They were usually, but not always, spoken.[39] Like other forms of magic, the Tudor charms are rooted in long-standing medieval traditions.[40] Although some scribes certainly adapted them after the Reformation to better accord with Protestant practice, many continued to employ the older religious formulae through the period. For more on this material, see in particular chapter 5.

Astrological images and rings derive largely from Arabic texts translated into Latin starting in the twelfth century. This literature overlaps in considerable measure with ritual magic in terms of its assumptions and practice (e.g., it might involve prayers to, and invocation of, planetary spirits) but was treated as a potential form of *naturalia* through the later Middle Ages. This literature assumes that, at the correct astrological moments, magical linkages may be forged with the power of the heavens through properly prepared "images." Images might include written or inscribed characters or actual figures and were understood to have ontological links with astral influences. The materials from which the images were formed, and which were used in their preparations (e.g., for suffumigation), were also key elements. Like ritual magic, this literature also was transmitted in the fifteenth and sixteenth centuries from its original setting in dedicated texts of astral magic such as the *Picatrix* into vernacular versions, often in books of "secrets" or "experiments." Such collections focused particularly on the natural properties of stones, herbs, and animals but might also include chemical, technological, or magical operations as well. In Tudor versions of such collections, ritual magic texts and astral magic are combined with a broader late medieval genre of secrets or experiments.[41] This is best exemplified by Sloane 3850 (Texts 3.6

39. Lea Olsan, "The Language of Charms in a Middle English Recipe Collection," *ANQ* 18 (2005): 29–35; "The Three Good Brothers Charm: Some Historical Points," *Incantatio* 1 (2011): 48–78.

40. Klaassen, *Making Magic*, 18–72.

41. On printed books of secrets, see William Eamon, *Science and the Secrets of Nature: Books of Secrets in Medieval*

and Early Modern Culture (Princeton: Princeton University Press, 1994); Allison Kavey, *Books of Secrets: Natural Philosophy in England, 1550–1600* (Urbana: University of Illinois Press, 2007). On the largely unexplored manuscript examples, see Laura Theresa Mitchell, "Cultural Uses of Magic in Fifteenth-Century England" (PhD thesis, University of Toronto, 2011).

and 4.4–4.6), a work that collects materials from natural, astral, and ritual magic.

Divination is the final form of magic to appear in these pages. Together with charms, divination was among the most common forms of magic practiced in medieval and early modern Europe, and like charms, most forms of divination appearing in manuscript have left no footprint in Tudor legal records. For example, we know of no legal documents concerned with divination for entertainment, love, potential misfortune, or medical purposes, some of which appear scattered in the magic texts below. However, Robert Allen's primary crime was divining the death date of the king. Practitioners also quite commonly appear in court for divining the identity of thieves.

Readers encountering premodern magic texts for the first time are often struck by the spirit names and words of power. The sense that these have arcane meanings or derive from earlier, potentially ancient, non-English sources is unsurprising since this was how they were intended to be understood. Indeed, some of these are very old. The earliest known instance of the "Sator Arepo" formula (see Text 4.4), for instance, was written on a wall in Pompeii. The most common words of power derive from the ninth-century *Alma Chorus Domini* and are either Latin or Latinized versions of Greek and Hebrew.[42] However, a large proportion of such words and names are entirely fanciful and no more than illustrations of what the authors of the texts thought they should sound or look like. We have included a table of the meanings of known words and the texts in which they occur as an appendix.

42. David Porreca, "Divine Names: A Cross-Cultural Comparison (Papyri Graecae Magicae, Picatrix, Munich Handbook)," *Magic, Ritual, and Witchcraft* 5 (2010): 19–29; Julien Véronèse, "God's Names and Their Uses in the Books of Magic Attributed to King Solomon," *Magic, Ritual, and Witchcraft* 5, no. 1 (2010): 30–50. See also "Alma Chorus Domini," in *Analecta hymnica Medii Aevii*, ed. G. M. Dreves and C. Blume, vols. 25 (no. 2) and 53 (no. 87), 55 vols. (Leipzig, 1886–1922).

NOTES ABOUT THE SOURCE MANUSCRIPTS

Although numerous manuscripts of magic survive from the Tudor period, our search for rituals matching those in the court cases did not always permit limiting ourselves to that period. As a result, the magic texts in this volume were written roughly between 1450 and 1650. We employed several volumes in the Sloane collection at the British Library. Sloane 3318 and 3846 are substantial early seventeenth-century volumes of magic texts. The first is in a single hand, the second collects material written by several scribes. Sloane 3849 contains several texts written in the sixteenth century, including the midcentury text from which we draw. Bodleian Library, e Mus. 173, is a collection of conjuring material from the early seventeenth century. Two of the books from which the texts in this volume have been drawn deserve special attention.

Additional B. 1 was collected sometime after the publication of Reginald Scot's *Discoverie of Witchcraft* (1584), from which it draws some material. This is a matter of some interest since Scot's work was explicitly antimagic and also profoundly hostile to Catholicism. The scribe evidently preferred the old religion (at least for the purposes of magic) and drew a number of such protective and healing charms from Scot. The work demonstrates the long life that medieval charms had in Tudor England and may well have been owned by a cunning person. Readers interested in this volume should refer to the full edition.[43]

Sloane 3850, fols. 143–66 (Texts 2.10, 3.6, and 4.5–4.7) is a collection entitled "Of Love, of Kardes, Dies and Tables, and Other Consaytes." It combines various magic experiments or secrets mostly focused on love, sex, invisibility, gambling, hunting, and fishing. It is executed in a messy hand with an artless title page, perhaps an attempt to emulate printed books. The scribe evidently liked magic that employed Latin phrases but had little knowledge of the language. As a result, the Latin portions are so full of mistakes as to make them difficult to read and sometimes incomprehensible. It also features a simple cipher replacing letters with numbers as follows:

---

43. Klaassen, *Making Magic.*

1	2	3	4	5	6	7	8	9
A	E	I	O	U/V	D	L	N/M	R

This cipher kept no secrets. Anyone of moderate intelligence could decipher it in a few minutes, and in any event, the scribe provided a key to it later in the same manuscript! Its purpose was rather to entertain or lend the text an aura of mystery or danger.

To give a sense of these colorful contents, the enciphered words have been included in parentheses in our text. Similarly, the botched Latin has generally been preserved in the text since the magic required that it be recited in that language. Translations (some of them conjectural) have been included in the notes.

EDITORIAL PRINCIPLES

This series emphasizes accessibility and readability for nonexperts. As a result (and with some hesitation) we have modernized spellings and punctuation. We have retained recognizable archaisms such as "thee" or "eth" verb endings (e.g., sendeth). We have retained a few important and frequently repeated archaic words, noting their meaning in the first occurrence. We have done the same in poetry, where this was often necessary to retain the rhyme scheme. Generally, however, where there is no modern cognate, we have replaced archaic words with modern equivalents and have placed the original word in the notes. Place-names (including parishes) have been identified by their modern names. The spelling of personal names has been made uniform throughout the text and rendered in modern equivalents where they exist. In the case of ciphers, we have decoded the original word in the text and have included the original cipher in parentheses. The titles of the texts generally have not been drawn from the manuscripts themselves but have been included for clarity and ease of reference.

In our presentation of English texts we have occasionally silently removed otiose conjunctions. Otherwise, we have maintained the word order of the original except in a few rare circumstances, in which case the original order is indicated in the notes. In all cases, where our readings are dubious or conjectural, we have provided the original text in the notes.

Latin texts have been translated into English, with some exceptions. In some instances, such as where formulae were meant to be spoken in Latin for their magical power, the Latin phrase has been maintained (e.g., *In nomine patris, et filii, et spiritus sancti*) and the meaning indicated at its first occurrence. Points where the manuscripts are in Latin have been indicated in the notes so readers will know the original language of the text and that the text is a translation rather than a modernized transcription. Where there is no note, readers may assume the original was in English. Translations of Latin have removed otiose repetitions of words like *dictus* (the said), which pepper legal Latin and render it confusing and cumbersome.

Occasionally, line breaks have been inserted or deleted for clarity and consistency. Points where the text shifts to a new page in the original manuscript are indicated with the folio/page number in square brackets. Where the original is damaged and cannot be read, such breaks are indicated in angle brackets and conjectural readings of missing letters or words are contained within them (e.g., sain<t . . .>).

Astrological sigils in the text have been expanded to their written equivalent (e.g., ☽ = moon; ☿ = Mercury). The line between magical figures and letters is often fuzzy. In general, where a line of magical letters is entirely decipherable, we have employed the modern letters. Where this is not the case, we have included graphic representations of the figures and/or letters.

CHAPTER 1

The God of Norfolk

Prognostication and Other Cunning

During the reign of King Edward VI a cunning man from Norfolk named Robert Allen was imprisoned in the Tower of London for using magic to predict the death of the young king.[1] There are no surviving trial records in Allen's case. However, a description of Allen's arrest in London is preserved in Edward Underhill's autobiography, to which are attached five scraps of parchment containing texts of magic and divination that were confiscated from Allen at the time of his arrest.[2] Also attached to Underhill's manuscript is a one-page record of an interrogation of Allen in the Tower of London by Sir John Godsalve in 1551. How these came to be with Underhill's manuscript is unclear. Together these records present a compelling picture of the Tudor demimonde of "ruffling roisters" that Underhill frequented as a younger man and in which he locates the activities of the cunning man Robert Allen in the late 1540s.

Since Edward Underhill's manuscript is the main source for Allen's activities, we need to provide some background for it. Underhill (b. 1512) came from a prominent Warwickshire family and rose to prominence as a courtier during the reign of Henry VIII. By his own account this period of his life was reprehensible. He passed the time with well-known gamblers at court. He spent a great deal of money, fell into debt, and humiliatingly had to sell his family estates at Hunningham in 1545.

1. Brian A. Harrison, *The Tower of London Prisoner Book* (Leeds: Royal Armouries, 2004), 171.

2. For sections transcribed here, see London, British Library, Harley 424 fols. 1r–8v and 425 fol. 98r–98v. See also George Lyman Kittredge, *Witchcraft in Old and New England* (New York: Russell & Russell, 1956), 229; John N. King, "Underhill, Edward (b. 1512, d. in or after 1576)," in *Oxford Dictionary of National Biography* (Oxford: Oxford University Press, 2010), https://doi.org/10.1093/ref:odnb/27997.

At some point, possibly wound up with losing his fortune, Underhill experienced a dramatic religious conversion: he embraced radical Protestantism and associated himself with similarly minded courtiers to Edward VI. It is from this perspective that Underhill describes Robert Allen's magical practices as threats to the Christian commonwealth. He finds it gravely problematic that the judicial system did not share his desire to firmly control the shifters, dicers, whore-hunters, and Catholics (his list) among whom he had squandered his youth.

Underhill's autobiography is undated; however, he refers to the fire that destroyed St. Paul's Cathedral, so it must have been composed after 1561 and before his death around 1576.[3] These dates mean it is possible that his memories about the events surrounding Robert Allen's arrest were as much as twenty-five years old when he recorded them. Although Underhill clearly remembers with relish his part in Allen's capture, his retelling of the event does not fit together perfectly in terms of chronology with other evidence, which is not surprising after the passing of time combined with Underhill's proclivity to use stories from his past for moralizing and self-aggrandizement.

The surviving body of evidence gives us a small window into Robert Allen's life and magic practice. The interrogation document and the loose parchment scraps containing texts for magical practice attached to the autobiography (presumably preserved by Underhill) provide some helpful dates and locations. That Allen came from Norfolk to London is supported by his epithet "the God of Norfolk" and by the statement of the Tower comptroller, Sir John Godsalve, who in 1539 had been constable of the castle and keeper of the jail at Norwich in Norfolk. Godsalve knew Allen by reputation if not in person at that time. In the 1551 interrogation record Godsalve indicated that Allen had been a practicing cunning man with a reputation for "judgments" (i.e., astrological prognostication). He had publicly predicted the arrest of Thomas Cromwell eleven days before it occurred in 1540 (although some would suggest this was simply stating the obvious).[4] For some reason Allen moved to London, perhaps to escape into anonymity,

3. John Gough Nichols, *Narratives of the Days of the Reformation* (London: Camden Society, 1859), 155.

4. Dale Hoak, "Godsalve, Sir John (b. in or before 1505, d. 1556)," in *Oxford Dictionary of National Biography* (Oxford: Oxford University Press, 2004).

perhaps to seek his fortune in the larger and wealthier client base offered by the big city. It is not clear whether the epithet was attached to him by his clients in Norfolk, invented by Allen to promote himself in London, or attributed to him ironically by his critics.

Robert Allen had operated as a cunning man in London for some years before being arrested, since Underhill recalled hearing about Allen as an established practitioner before his own conversion, which was sometime after 1545 and before 1547. Some aspects of Underhill's report seem dubious, such as his claim that Allen's clients were mostly women. Underhill contradicts himself in this claim when he recounts being told by his acquaintance, the "great dicer" Morgan of Salisbury Court, that Allen knew how "to make a woman love a man, to teach men how to win at the dice, and what should become of this realm." This, on balance, suggests a male rather than female clientele. Text 1.4 below confirms that gambling magic was one of his specialties. Allen's only named client was also a man, a lawyer called Gastone, who seems to have supported Allen on an ongoing basis and to have provided him with a room. Much of Underhill's account suggests that he wanted to play up the dysfunctional nature of Gastone's household as the scene of regular debauchery of one kind or another. Underhill insinuates that the household was supported by female clients paying for magical assistance "to blear their husbands' eyes withall." Naturally, there is no reason to doubt that many of Allen's clients may have been women, and these women appear to have been clients of Gastone's "old wife," but Underhill's emphasis on them may have been an effort to denigrate or shame Allen by association with ungoverned women.

Underhill also wrote that Allen's arrest provoked animosity toward himself among Gastone's friends, whom he describes as "lords and ladies, gentlemen, merchants, knaves, whores, bauds, and thieves." To his chagrin these "friends" were responsible for ensuring that Allen ultimately went free. As is by now clear, there is some dramatization in this story; however, as cases in this book and the work of Owen Davies make clear, successful cunning folk did have a loyal and dedicated clientele.[5] Thus, it may well be that the story is more accurate

---

5. Davies, *Cunning-Folk*, 13–14. See also Macfarlane, *Witchcraft in Tudor and Stuart England*, 115–30. The case of Thomas Fansome (Text 3.5) demonstrates the importance of testimonial letters for practitioners.

than it first appears and that Allen did indeed have powerful allies at all levels of society who were entirely happy with the magic services that he provided.

Allen was not arrested for magic, however. Instead, his arrest was prompted by his prediction regarding the death of King Edward VI. The Tower of London's record states: "Robart Alen. Committed before 31 October [1551] charged with predicting Edward VI would die within a year. Sentenced to a year in prison. Still in custody at the end of the account period ending 1 May 1552."[6] How long before October 31, 1551, Allen had been committed to the Tower and what was the date of his sentencing are impossible to say without trial records.

According to Underhill's version of events, Allen was arrested because of a "bruit in the city that the king was dead, which I [i.e., Underhill] declared to the mayor, requiring him to have an officer apprehend him."[7] Underhill specifically names Sir John Gresham as the mayor to whom he reported Allen, and this creates a temporal problem because John Gresham was mayor of London only in 1547.[8] The rumors of Edward VI's death, however, were two years later in the summer of 1549 and were clearly recorded by the young king in his diary for that year.[9] Underhill went on to state that he accompanied the mayor's officers to St. Paul's, where they arrested Allen and took him to the lord protector. The only lord protector during Edward's reign was Edward Seymour, Duke of Somerset, and, although Seymour was removed and arrested in October of 1549, he was still active in the summer of 1549 around the time of the rumors. Underhill further stated that the lord protector had him take Allen to the Tower and provided a letter to the lieutenant of the Tower, whom he names as

6. Harrison, *Tower of London Prisoner Book*, 171. See also John Whitcomb Bayley, *The History and Antiquities of the Tower of London, with Memoirs of Royal and Distinguished Persons* (London: T. Cadell, 1825), 2:xlvi.

7. A bruit is a malicious rumor.

8. John's brother Richard was mayor before him. Ian Blanchard, "Gresham, Sir Richard (c. 1485–1549), Mercer, Merchant Adventurer, and Mayor of London," in *Oxford*

Dictionary of National Biography (Oxford: Oxford University Press, 2008), https://doi.org/10.1093/ref:odnb /11504.

9. Edward's London excursion was July 3, 1549. See W. K. Jordan, ed., *Chronicle and Political Papers* (Ithaca: Cornell University Press, 1966), 13; Jonathan North, ed., *England's Boy King: The Diary of Edward VI, 1547–1553* (Welwyn Garden City, UK: Ravenhall, 2005), 32.

Sir John Markham. Markham was appointed to that office in 1549.[10] So the greater part of Underhill's story points to Allen's arrest in 1549 and not 1547, when Gresham was mayor.

An arrest date of 1549 also works with the interrogation in 1551 by Sir John Godsalve, who was comptroller of the Tower mint from June 24, 1548, to March 25, 1552. If Underhill's description is *mostly* accurate, that would mean Allen was held in the Tower for nearly three years, from the summer of 1549 till at least 1552. Unfortunately, there are many points upon which Underhill introduces other possibilities through inconsistencies in his narrative, such as stating that it was about a year before Allen was released through the help of friends.

More important than the date of Allan's imprisonment is the issue of why he was released at all and not executed for treasonous and felonious prognostication on the king's death. From the early fifteenth century, political prophecy had been prohibited by law, due to its potential to inspire rebellion.[11] Laws were enacted to prevent prophecy by Henry IV (1402 and 1406), Henry VIII (1541–42), Edward VI (1549–50 and 1552–53), and, after the period under consideration here, Elizabeth (1562–63 and 1580–81).[12] Prophesying the king's death was particularly dangerous since it carried the additional weight of treason. Under Henry VIII the Treasons Act of 1534 made any discussion of the king's death a treasonable offense, and in 1542 an Act "Touchyng Prophecies uppon Declaracion of Names, Armes, Badges and etc." made political prophecy a felony.[13]

10. Alan Cameron, "Markham, Sir John (b. before 1486, d. 1559), Soldier and Member of Parliament," in *Oxford Dictionary of National Biography* (Oxford: Oxford University Press, 2004), https://doi.org/10.1093/ref:odnb/37736.

11. Ethan H. Shagan, "Rumours and Popular Politics in the Reign of Henry VIII," in *The Politics of the Excluded, c. 1500–1850*, ed. Tim Harris (Basingstoke, UK: Palgrave, 2001), 30–66. For a broad discussion of political prophecy, see Young, *Magic as a Political Crime*.

12. See *Rotuli Parliamentorum*, III, 508 item 90 (against entertainers, vagabonds, and divinators) and 583 item 62 (against the Lollards); Statutes of the Realm, 33 Hen VIII. c. 14; 3 and 4 Edw. VI c. 15; 7 Edw. VI c. 11; 5 Eliz. c. 15; 23 Eliz. c. 2.

13. John G. Bellamy, *The Tudor Law of Treason: An Introduction*, Studies in Social History (London: Routledge & Kegan Paul, 1979), 31; Sharon L. Jansen, *Political Protest and Prophecy Under Henry VIII* (Woodbridge, UK: Boydell Press, 1991), 60–61; David Cressy, *Dangerous Talk: Scandalous, Seditious, and Treasonable Speech in Pre-modern England* (Oxford: Oxford University Press, 2010), 39–60.

Given this context, Allen was quite fortunate, especially after being found (according to Underhill) with incriminating evidence of prognostication of the king's death chalked on the floor of his rooms. When Markham interrogated Allen in Underhill's presence, the cunning man thought that the repeal of Henry's antimagic legislation made his activities legal. While Allen was wrong about this, it reveals that he was aware of the laws governing his profession. Some knowledge of the law and friends like the lawyer Gastone could have gone a long way to easing his situation. It is possible that Allen was charged with misprision of treason (not reporting knowledge of treasonous plans) instead of treason and was therefore imprisoned at the king's pleasure rather than given a capital sentence;[14] this could explain his long imprisonment and ultimate release (if we are to accept Underhill's story that he *was* released).[15] Kett's rebellion in the same summer of 1549 must also have offered a major distraction to Edward IV's officials. In the face of such a large uprising, it would be easy to overlook Allen's magical prognostication as a petty threat and leave him moldering in the Tower.[16]

Of the five magic texts seized by Underhill and set out below, three are written in entirely different hands and two in an identical hand. It seems likely that two texts written in the same hand (the astrological fragments, Texts 1.6 and 1.7) are Allen's autographs, for the following reasons. In his interrogation, Allen boasts of being a better astrologer than the masters at Oxford, an opinion that was not shared by the expert consulted in this case, the well-known polymath Robert Recorde.[17] Nonetheless, astrology was clearly one of Allen's specialties. The horary astrological chart, which is always personal

14. Bellamy, *Tudor Law of Treason*, 52–53.

15. Dobin says Allen was executed in 1551. He cites Kittredge, who makes no such claim. See Howard Dobin, *Merlin's Disciples: Prophecy, Poetry, and Power in Renaissance England* (Stanford: Stanford University Press, 1990), 1; Kittredge, *Witchcraft in Old and New England*, 230.

16. D. MacCulloch, "Kett's Rebellion in Context," *Past and Present* 84 (1979): 36–59; Ethan H. Shagan, "Protector Somerset and the 1549 Rebellions: New Sources and New Perspectives," *English Historical Review* 114 (1999): 34–63.

17. Gareth Roberts and Fenny Smith, eds., *Robert Recorde: The Life and Times of a Tudor Mathematician* (Cardiff: University of Wales Press, 2012).

and specific, would have been cast for a particular client seeking an answer to a very specific question. It is the sort of thing that would have had no value to Allen unless he had prepared it for a client. The works on the other pieces of parchment would have been useful to anyone and could easily have been collected by Allen from other cunning folk. Such trade in magic equipment and texts was not unusual, and similar one-sheet fragments containing a single magic operation survive from this period.[18]

The fragments preserved by Underhill, Allen's boasts while in the Tower, the chalked predictions on Allen's floor, and his reputation for astrological judgments all suggest that his cunning lay in astrology. This makes him singular among the cunning folk examined in this volume. At the same time, astrology, astrological prediction, and prophecy were also practiced by other cunning folk in the period, and Underhill's account makes clear he also specialized in magic for love and gambling.[19] The record also suggests that Allen had magic books like other cunning folk, but there is no indication what they were or what may have happened to them.

EXPLICATION OF ROBERT ALLEN'S ONOMANCY (TEXT 1.5)

Onomancy is a form of divination based on a person's name. The text is far from clear, but this is our best guess as to how it was supposed to work. We employ the second method in Text 1.5 as our example since it is the most clearly articulated and suggests the probable interpretation of the first and third methods. The question we pose is whether Frank and Sharon should go on pilgrimage. For the sake of simplicity, we use only first names, although the text requires surnames as well.

18. On the sharing of texts among cunning folk, see Klaassen and Wright, *Magic of Rogues*, 5, 14–16, 30, and 143. For magic text on a single folded sheet, see Washington, Folger Shakespeare Library, Xd 234, and Frederika Bain, "The Binding of the Fairies: Four Spells," *Preternature* 1, no. 2 (2012): 323–54.

19. Klaassen and Wright, *Magic of Rogues*, 12–13, 21–55, and 62–63.

Typically, a numerical value is assigned to each letter in the name. It seems likely they would be numbered in a manner something like this:

a	b	c	d	e	f	g	h	i/j	k	l	m	n	o	p	q	r	s	t	u/v	w	x	y	z
1	2	3	4	5	6	7	8	9	10	11	12	13	14	15	16	17	18	19	20	21	22	23	24

The numerical values of the letters in our names would add up to 117 (Frank = 6 + 17 + 1 + 13 + 10 and Sharon = 18 + 8 + 17 + 14 + 13). To this we would add 67, the numerical value of Monday, the day we plan to depart (i.e., 12 +14 + 13 + 4 + 1 + 23), and the number of that day in the lunar month. (This would start from the new moon.) Let us say the Monday of our departure was the tenth day in the lunar month. An additional 30 would be added to that. Hence, 117 +67 + 10 + 30 = 224. Twenty-five would then be repeatedly subtracted from 224 until it was not possible to subtract more (i.e., 8 times). This would render the number 24. Since this is an even number, our trip would fare well.

The first and third methods seem likely to have used the same basic procedure. To determine if Frank was lying when he spoke on a Monday, 30 should be added to numerical value of his name and of Monday. It makes most sense that 25 was supposed to be repeatedly subtracted until it was not possible to subtract more, and the final number evaluated. Similarly, in the third method, one would arrive at the final number by adding together the numerical value of the person's name, the name of the benefice (i.e., the name of the parish), and the value of the day (or perhaps the day of the lunar month). From this 30 would be repeatedly subtracted as in the above methods.

THE TEXTS

1.1. ROBERT ALLEN IN THE TOWER OF LONDON
(FROM THE AUTOBIOGRAPHY OF EDWARD UNDERHILL)[20]

This Luke [Shepherd] wrote many proper books against the papists, for the which he was imprisoned in the Fleet, especially a book called *John Boone and Mast Parsone*, who reasoned together of the natural presence in the sacrament, which book he wrote in the time of King Edward, wherewith the papists were sore grieved, especially Sir John Gresham, then being mayor.[21] John Daye did print the same book, who the mayor sent for to know the maker thereof, saying he should also go to prison for printing of the same.

It was my chance to come in the same time, for that I had found out where Allen the prophesier had a chamber, through whom there was a bruit[22] in the city that the king was dead, which I declared to the mayor, requiring him to have an officer apprehend him.

"Marry," said the mayor, "I have received letters this night at midnight to make search for the such." He was going unto dinner and[23] willed me to take part of the same. As we were at dinner, he said there was a book put forth called John Boone, the maker whereof he would also search for.

"Why so?" said I. "That book is a good book. I have one of them here and there are[24] many of them in the court."

"Have you so?" said he. "I pray you, let me see it, for I have not seen any of them." So he took it and read a little of it, and laughed thereat, as it was both pithy and merry. By means wherof, John Day, sitting at the sideboard after dinner, was bidden go home who had else gone to prison.[25] [fol. 98v.]

When we had dined, the mayor sent two of his officers with me to seek Allen, whom we met with in St. Paul's,[26] and took him with us unto

20. London, British Library, Harley 425, fol. 98r–98v and Harley 424, fol. 8r–8v.

21. An anti-Catholic satire by Luke Shepherd, *John Bon and Mast Person* was published by the evangelical printer John Day in either 1547 or 1548. The British Library dates it to 1548.

Gresham was mayor in 1547, which suggests this was the correct date.

22. I.e., a malicious rumor.

23. *who*

24. *is*

25. I.e., John Day otherwise would have gone to prison.

26. *Poles*

his chamber, where we found figures set to chalk, the [astrological] nativity of the king, and a judgment given of his death. Whereof this foolish wretch thought himself so sure that he and his counsellors, the papists, bruited it all over. The king lay at Hampton Court, the same time, and my lord protector at Syon,[27] unto whom I carried this Allen with his books of conjurations, circles, and many things belonging to that devilish art which he affirmed before me to be lawful science, for the statute against such was repealed.[28]

"Thou foolish knave," said my Lord, "if thou and all that be of thy science tell me what I shall do tomorrow, I will give thee all that I have." Commanding me to carry him unto the Tower, he wrote a letter unto Sir John Markham, then being lieutenant, to cause him to be examined by such as were learned.[29]

Mr. Markham, as he was both wise and zealous in the Lord, talked with him, unto whom he [Allen] did affirm that he knew more in the science of astronomy than all the universities of Oxford and Cambridge. Whereupon he sent for my friend, before spoken of, Doctor Recorde,[30] who examined him and he [Allen] knew not the rules of astronomy but was a very unlearned ass and a sorcerer. For this he was worthy [of] hanging, said Mr. Recorde.

To have further matter unto him we sent for Thomas Robins, [Harley 424, fol. 8r] alias Morgan, commonly called little Morgan or Tom Morgan, brother unto great Morgan, of Salisbury court, the great dicer, who, when I was a companion with them, told me many stories of this Allen, what a cunning man he was, and what things he could do, as to make a woman love a man, to teach men how to win at the dice, and what should become of this realm—[there was] nothing but he knew it. He [Allen] had his chambers in diverse places of the city,

27. Edward Seymour, Duke of Somerset. Arrested in 1549.

28. This refers to the repealing of Henry VIII's antimagic legislation by Edward VI in 1547. It demonstrates that cunning folk, at least in London, were aware of the law.

29. Markham was appointed Lieutenant to the Tower in 1549 and

was relieved of this duty in 1551 due to overly indulgent treatment of prisoners.

30. Doctor Robert Recorde (d. 1558), Oxford- and Cambridge-trained physician and mathematician and personal doctor to Edward VI and Queen Mary Tudor. NA PROB 11/40/313.

whither resorted many women for things stolen or lost, to know their fortunes, and their children's fortunes, where the ruffling roisters, the dicers, made their matches.

When this Morgan and Allen were brought together, Morgan utterly denied that ever he had seen him or known him.

"Yes," said Allen, "You know me and I know you." For he had confessed that before his coming. Upon this, Mr. Lieutenant [John Markham] stayed Little Morgan also as an accomplice[31] in the Tower. I caused also Mr. Gastone, the lawyer, who was also a great dicer, to be apprehended, in whose house Allen was much and had a chamber there where many things were practiced.[32] Gastone had an old wife who was laid under the table[33] all night for dead and when the women in the morning came to wind her,[34] they found that there was life in her and they recovered her. And she lived about two years after by the resort of such as came to seek for things stolen and lost which they would hide for the nonce, to blear their husbands' eyes withal, saying the wise man told them.[35] Of such [people] Gastone had chosen for himself, and his friends, young lawyers of the Temple. Thus I became so despised and odious unto the lawyers, lords and ladies, gentlemen, merchants, knaves, whores, bawds, and thieves, that I walked as dangerously as Daniel amongst the lions. [fol. 8v] Yet from them all, the Lord delivered me, notwithstanding their frequent[36] devices and conspiracies by violence to have shed my blood, or with sorcery [to have] destroyed me. These aforesaid were in the Tower about the space of a year and then by friendship delivered. So scapeth always the wicked, and such as God commandeth should not live among the people. Yea, even now in these days also, so that me think I see the ruin of London and this whole realm to be even at hand, for God will not suffer any longer. Love is clean banished. No man is sorry for Joseph's hurt.[37]

---

31. *personar*

32. *where was many thinges practesed*

33. *board*

34. = wound in a shroud for burial

35. This suggests that Gastone's wife was also a practicing cunning woman.

36. *oftone*

37. This refers to the biblical story of Joseph, who was sold into slavery by his brothers.

1.2. NOTES FROM ALLEN'S INTERROGATION[38]

Memorandum, that Allen requireth to talk with one of the council, saying if he were unburdened of that which he would then say, he cared not what became of him.

Also, he saith afore the commissioners that he can make the great elixir.

Also, he stood earnestly before the said commissioners that he could say more concerning astrology and astronomy than all the learned men within the universities of Oxford and Cambridge. And yet [he] understands no part of the Latin tongue.

Item Sir John Godsalve required the commissioners to demand whether that Allen did not say unto two men yet living that eleven days before the apprehension of the Lord Cromwell, that the said Lord Cromwell should be in the tower within fourteen days following.

Item the question being demanded of him, he denied not that he said so, but said that he spoke it not of his own knowledge but of others.

Item Sir John Godsalve sayeth that he was born in Norfolk, and that he had been a great doer in judgments of diverse matters there.

This Allen was called the God of Norfolk before they received the light of the gospel.[39]

Allen's Confiscated Papers

1.3. FOR THEFT[40]

If a man has stolen any thing of thine.
Take and write in parchment + Agios + Agios + Agios + Crux Crux Crux spiritus sanctus spiritus sanctus spiritus[41] be El the servant of God. And put it over the head and the same night thou shalt know who it is. [fol. 2]

---

38. London, British Library, Harley 424, fol. 7r.

39. This final sentence is in Underhill's handwriting.

40. London, British Library, Harley 424, fols. 1–2.

41. The Latin words are "cross" and "Holy Spirit."

If any manner of woman have done the theft.

Take and write these names in virgin wax + Agios + Agios + Agios + and hold it in thy left hand under thy right ear and lay thee to sleep and thou shalt have a vision and knowledge [of] who hath thy thing.

1.4. FOR GAMBLING[42]

When thou wilt go forth to play at the cards and dice, let the ascendant be in a sign movable as Aries, Cancer, Libra, [or] Leo.[43] And let the lord of the ascendant be well disposed in a good place. And let the seventh house be feeble and impedite.[44] And if it may be, let the lord of the eighth house be in the second or first house received of the lord of the second or the first house, nor let not him receive the lord of the second. And let the moon be she separate from a fortune and joining to another fortune fortunate and strong. And let not her be upon the earth.

And the breast of the player toward the moon and his face. And if all these things cannot be done, at the least see [that] it be a movable sign when thou goest out for to play and [that] the moon [be] upon thy breast when thou playest. Or at the least, see that thy breast and face be toward the moon.

1.5. ONOMANCY[45]

And if thou will be certain[46] whether a man tells ye a false tale or true, take the letters of his name and of his surname and of that day. And put to all the number thirty. And then depart all that whole number by twenty-five. And if there leave[47] [an] even number at the last end, it is false that he telleth and if it be odd it is true.

And if thou will be certain,[48] when going [on] a pilgrimage, whether they shall well go and come back without harm or not, take the number of the letters of their names and of the day and of the age of the moon and the name of the place that they go to, and put to all these thirty and then depart all the whole numbers by twenty-five as

---

42. London, British Library, Harley 424, fol. 3.

43. The last sigil is poorly written and may be Capricorn instead of Leo.

44. = obstructed

45. London, British Library, Harley 424, fol. 4.

46. *wette*

47. = there remains

48. *wette*

long as ye may. And if there leave an even number, they shall go and come without hurt or harm. And if the number be odd they shall not speed well.

And [in] this manner you may know[49] all manner of things that you desire.

Also, if you will be certain[50] of a man that want to have a benefice or to go to religion [i.e., become a priest],[51] take the letters of his name and of the benefice and of the day and depart them by thirty. And if there leave [an] even number, he shall speed. And if there leave [an] odd he shall not speed. And if there leave nine he shall be religious.

1.6. HORARY ASTROLOGICAL CHART[52]

Note: We deviate from our usual editorial practice here and include a reproduction of this page (Fig. 1) since it appears to have been written in Robert Allen's own hand. We include a transcription of the text below.

The center of the chart reads, "The moon separate from a sextile of Mars applying to a square of Saturn, lord of the hour Jupiter."

The text below reads, "Whether it is better to remove or to continue where the querant[53] do dwell still and whether they be past danger of [the] burning of their house or goods or not."

1.7. LIST OF PROPITIOUS ASTROLOGICAL TIMES[54]

If thou wilt take a journey to do anything.

The moon being in Aries, go in the hour [of] Mars.
The moon in Taurus, go in the hour of Venus.
The moon in Gemini, go in the hour [of] Venus.
The moon in Cancer, go in the hour of the moon.
The moon in Leo, go in the hour of the sun.
The moon in Virgo, go in the hour of Mercury.
The moon in Scorpio, go in the hour of Mars.
The moon in Capricorn, go in the hour of Saturn.

49. *wette*
50. *wette*
51. I.e., become a priest.
52. London, British Library, Harley 424, fol. 5.
53. = questioner
54. London, British Library, Harley 424, fol. 6.

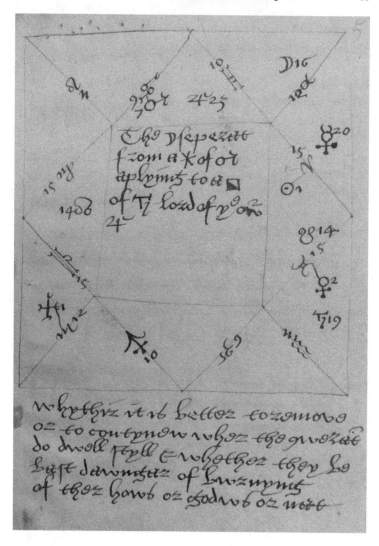

FIGURE 1 John Foxe's papers, volume 9, sixteenth–seventeenth century, "Astrological scheme resolving whether it is better to remove or to contynew where the qwerant do dwell styll and whether they be past dawnger of burnyng of ther hows or godws or nat." London, British Library, Harley MS 424, fol. 5r. © British Library Board, 2021. Photo © The Granger Collection Ltd d/b/a GRANGER Historical Picture Archive.

The moon in Aquarius, go in the hour of Saturn.
The moon in Pisces, go in the hour of Jupiter.[55]

Note: When the moon is in Gemini, go not in the hour [of] the sun.
When the moon is in Pisces, go not in the hour [of] Mercury
When the moon is in Virgo, go not in the hour of Venus.
When the moon is in Cancer, go not in the hour [of] Mars.
And so forth [with] all [the] others.

55. Each hour of the day was associated with a planet.

CHAPTER 2

Theft Divination and the Return of Stolen Goods

William Wycherly, a merchant tailor and cunning man working in London, was examined in the ecclesiastical courts in 1549. Wycherly's signed confession said that he had used key-and-psalter magic for identifying thieves "so often that he ... cannot expresse how many the tymes." He claimed that so many people pressed him to perform this kind of magic that he had to hide indoors to avoid them.[1] Wycherly also confessed to using conjuring circles and crystals to summon spirits to help him find lost and stolen goods, and he maintained there were more than five hundred practicing conjurers in England. Like so many defendants, Wycherly was careful to frame his confession in a way that downplayed its gravity by emphasizing its commonplace nature and painting himself as an unwilling magician overwhelmed by people pleading for help. Nonetheless, he was correct that many people wanted theft divination performed and that it was regularly practiced throughout England.

Theft was an enormous problem in premodern society, and English legal historians have found that property offenses made up nearly three-quarters of the felonies prosecuted in early modern secular courts.[2] Given the prevalence of theft, it should come as no

---

1. London, BL, MS Lansdowne 2/26. Nichols, *Narratives*, 332; Kittredge, *Witchcraft in Old and New England*, 197; Davies, *Cunning-Folk*, 5, 94, and 100.

2. Garthine Walker, *Crime, Gender and Social Order in Early Modern England*, Cambridge Studies in Early Modern British History (Cambridge: Cambridge University Press, 2003); J. M. Beattie, "The Pattern of Crime in England," *Past and Present* 62 (1974): 73–78; J. S. Cockburn, "The Nature and Incidence of Crime in England,

1559–1625," in *Crime in England, 1550–1800*, ed. J. S. Cockburn (Princeton: Princeton University Press, 1977), 60–70; Cynthia B. Herrup, *The Common Peace: Participation and the Criminal Law in Seventeenth-Century England*, Cambridge Studies in Early Modern British History (Cambridge: Cambridge University Press, 1987), 45–47; J. A. Sharpe, *Crime in Seventeenth-Century England: A County Study*, 2nd ed., Past and Present Publications (London: Longman, 1999), 91–92.

surprise that magic for identifying thieves or stolen goods was an everyday activity of cunning folk and very frequent in both manuscripts and legal documents. Many people turned to magic when their goods were stolen.

The theft of a silver spoon or a set of beads might seem like a small matter, but most premodern people had few luxury items in their household, and those they did possess were highly prized for emotional and financial reasons. Movable property (chattels) frequently passed with brides into new households as part of women's dowries. These items might well be heirlooms and were regarded as part of a family's legacy for future children as well as for supporting a wife in her widowhood, which was likely to be the poorest part of her life. For this reason, the theft of household items must have been particularly enraging for women, who, due to English property law, rarely owned land and often had a limited number of personal possessions they could legally call their own.[3] In the cases included in this chapter, many women who were the victims of theft turned to magic to find the thief (Texts 2.3, 2.5, and 2.6). Men also pursued thieves in this way (Texts 2.1 and 2.4).[4]

The close-knit nature of late medieval and early modern communities meant that accusing someone of theft through the courts was complicated. Many victims of theft and those they suspected knew one another and were bound together in various ways, either as master and servant, friends and family, or neighbors living in the same parish. Theft of an item worth 12 pence or more (grand larceny) was a felony punishable by hanging. As much as someone might hate their thieving neighbor, making a formal accusation was a complicated matter. It must have been hard to feel responsible (or to be blamed by other members of your community) for bringing about a person's

3. Janet S. Loengard, "'Which May Be Said to Be Her Own': Widows and Goods in Late-Medieval England," in *Medieval Domesticity: Home, Housing and Household in Medieval England*, ed. Maryanne Kowaleski and P. J. P. Goldberg (Cambridge: Cambridge University Press, 2008); Loengard, "Plate, Good Stuff, and Household Things': Husbands, Wives, and Chattels in England at the End of the Middle Ages," in *Tant D'emprises = So Many Undertakings: Essays in Honour of Anne F. Sutton*, ed. Livia Visser-Fuchs ([Upminster, Essex]: Richard III Society, 2003).

4. See also Klaassen and Wright, *Magic of Rogues*, 24, 39, 85, 90–94, and 100; Davies, *Cunning-Folk*, 5, 94, and 100.

death. In his study of crime in parishes, Sharp found that pressure could be placed on complainants to reduce the claimed value of stolen goods to 11 pence or less (petty larceny) in order to save the life of a locally known thief.[5]

An additional disincentive for resorting to the courts to prosecute a thief was the almost certain loss of the stolen item, especially before 1529, because a guilty verdict resulted in the forfeiture of the stolen goods to the crown.[6] After 1529 a statute issued by Henry VIII made it possible, although not easy, for plaintiffs to petition for the return of their stolen goods if the thief was found guilty.[7] The requirement of petitioning the courts added time and cost to the process of recovery.

In light of both premodern community life and the inflexibility of the common law, the frequent resort to magical theft detection is much easier to understand. Paying a cunning person surely cost less than court fees and did not risk the major social disruption that a hanging might provoke. Moreover, the victim stood a better chance of having the item returned if the magical process correctly identified the thief, who understandably could be pressured into a private settlement rather than hazarding the courts.

Extralegal self-help could create its own problems, however. Angry victims who believed they had identified their thief with the help of a cunning practitioner might have little compunction about taking vengeance into their own hands. In some cases, this could be done by means of magic, as we see in Text 2.9, which employs wax images to torture identified thieves. It could also lead to gossip and public accusation. These were themselves significant vehicles of strife within a community, potentially destroying reputations and bringing about lifelong animosities.[8] The accused often resorted to the courts to clear their name after suffering substantial reputational harm, as

5. Sharpe, *Crime*, 88–90 and 110–11; Gregory Durston, *Crime and Justice in Early Modern England: 1500–1750* (Chichester, UK: Barry Rose Law, 2004), 38, 322.

6. K. J. Kesselring, "Felony Forfeiture in England, c.1170–870," *Journal of Legal History* 30, no. 3 (2009): 201–26; Kesselring, "Felony Forfeiture and the Profits of Crime in Early Modern

England," *Historical Journal* 53 (2010): 271–88.

7. Great Britain, *Statutes of the Realm*, 21 Henry VIII, c. 11.

8. See, for example, Sandy Bardsley, *Venomous Tongues: Speech and Gender in Late Medieval England* (Philadelphia: University of Pennsylvania Press, 2006).

the case of Elizabeth Doland (Text 2.5) demonstrates. We learn about the use of magical divination in her case because she complained to the bishop of London's officials that John White had publicly defamed her as a thief, after which her husband beat her and threw her out of the house. In similar cases, Alice Anceyr (Text 2.6) and Sir Robert the Rector (Text 2.4) were presented for defamation because they had accused people of stealing their property, putatively having used magic to identify them.[9]

The manuscripts record a wide number of methods for identifying thieves, many of which do not appear in legal records. The most frequently recorded operation for thief detection in late medieval and early modern England (Text 2.7 and 2.10) is commonly referred to as "the Eye of Abraham."[10] Despite its frequent presence in manuscript, it is not attested at all in court records. The same applies to the other methods appearing in Texts 3.8, 3.10, and 3.13. By contrast, the key-and-psalter method of divination (Texts 3.11 and 3.12) is considerably *less* common in manuscripts despite being attested often in court records.[11] It seems likely that the latter technique did not derive from learned traditions and was only absorbed into magic manuscripts toward the end of the sixteenth century, at which time collectors of magic material became more interested in popular traditions.

No doubt, the key-and-psalter method was used more frequently simply because it was more practical. Although the technique in the Eye of Abraham of lining up the accused, intimidating them with an arcane ritual, and ultimately magically inflicting dire pain upon them made for a powerful fantasy of revenge, private investigation through magic was far more manageable and easily arranged. Both the key-and-psalter method and scrying to see the thief in a stone or mirror

9. For a case complaining of false arrest for the theft based on scrying with a child and glass, see NA C/1/307/41. See also Derek Neal, "Suits Make the Man: Masculinity in Two English Law Courts, c. 1500," *Canadian Journal of History* 37 (April 2002): 9.

10. Other manuscript examples include London, British Library, Additional 34111, fol. 75r; Sloane 3846, fol. 41r; Sloane 3846, fol. 83r–v; Sloane 3542, fol. 19r.

11. Scot also describes the process in Reginald Scot, *The Discouerie of Witchcraft* (London: W. Brome, 1584), XII, v.

were practiced more or less in private and did not require the thief to be present.

In the key-and-psalter method, the operator wrote the names of those suspected on scraps of paper and each of these was then subjected to the test. A scrap containing a name was rolled and inserted into the hollow stem of a key. The key was then laid in a psalter with the key resting on Psalm 49, part of which reads, "If thou sawest a theefe thou diddest consent unto him." The key was then clamped into the book using the hasps commonly attached to premodern book covers. The operator and the client then suspended the book, each placing one finger under one side of the rounded end of the key. (See the illustration in Text 2.12, which clearly shows two right hands.) If the psalter turned and fell to the ground while they held it aloft, the person whose name was written on the scrap of paper was deemed to be the guilty party. A poor man's version of this was the sieve-and-shears method, in which the operators suspended a sieve (turned sideways) by means of a set of shears clamped around its rim. Both techniques are widely attested.[12]

Key-and-psalter divination would have been convincing for several reasons. First, as in Text 2.11, it might be accompanied by conventional religious exercises and might even have been performed by a priest. This, combined with the use of one of the most important books in the Bible—one used in every religious ritual—would have imbued the ritual with legitimacy and authenticity. Second, while it is relatively easy to suspend a book in this manner from one's own fingers, it is more difficult to do so with two people. So it required the close attention of both the operator and his client. Third, that

---

12. For English examples, see Klaassen and Wright, *Magic of Rogues*, 108; Klaassen, *Making Magic*, 58; Kittredge, *Witchcraft in Old and New England*, 45, 186, and 96–99. For a Germanic example, see Edward Watts Morton Bever, *The Realities of Witchcraft and Popular Magic in Early Modern Europe: Culture, Cognition, and Everyday Life* (New York: Palgrave Macmillan, 2008), 224. Peter of Abano's mention of it attests to Italian use. Lynn Thorndike, *A History of Magic and Experimental Science*, 8 vols. (New York: Macmillan, 1923–50), 2:903. For Iberia and Brazil, see Laura de Mello e Souza, *The Devil and the Land of the Holy Cross: Witchcraft, Slavery, and Popular Religion in Colonial Brazil*, trans. Diane Grosklaus Whitty (Austin: University of Texas Press, 2003), 95–96.

attentiveness would have been rewarded by an eerie sense that the book had a motive force of its own. The considerable mass of the book hanging on a pivot point made it unstable to hold. A slight movement in either direction could result in a dramatic torque that could seem to have been caused by the book rather than either of those holding it. Finally, as is the case with the modern Ouija board, the tool would not have been convincing if it were obviously manipulated by a single person. Consequently, it may not have been obvious who had caused the psalter to turn, and, more interestingly, that turning might well have been the result of the combined and unintentional movements of the participants.[13]

This linking of two or more people in a kind of creative process of divination is perhaps best illustrated in the process of scrying, also used in theft detection (Texts 2.1, 2.3, and 2.6). In this method, one person, usually known as the master, performs magical rites over a stone, crystal, or mirror, rendering it a kind of spiritual portal in which visions of spirits or past events may be seen. Another person, the scryer, then looks into the object to see spirits or a vision.[14] In some cases, the operator was also the scryer and worked with a client who may or may not have been directly involved in the magic rituals. Modern studies suggests that, with the right psychological conditioning or training, a significant portion of the population can experience visual or auditory hallucinations.[15] But this was only part of what made it potentially convincing.

In this form of magic, the answers to the questions sought resulted from a complex process involving the interactions of information provided by the master or client, the questions they might ask, and the visions or creative inventions of the scryer. The persistence of this dynamic in modern divination techniques such as Tarot, or even the practices of internet psychics, attests to its potentially convincing nature. Among the court documents, Nazareth Jarbrey (perhaps the

---

13. Bever, *Realities of Witchcraft,* 221–50.

14. For another example of a court case involving theft detection using a child scryer, see NA C/1/307/41.

15. Bever, *The Realities of Witchcraft,* 235–50. On modern religion, see T. M. Luhrmann, *When God Talks Back: Understanding the American Evangelical Relationship with God* (New York: Alfred A. Knopf, 2012).

earliest recorded female scryer) and Thomas Barley divided their duties as master and scryer (Text 2.3). This case also reveals an additional level of creative interaction. When Nazareth described the thief whom she observed, a third person (a cleric) identified the thief based on her description. On the surface it might appear that the critical mechanism in this form of magic was simply for the magician to provide a compelling vision. However, the mechanisms of this form of magic included a process that, as Deborah Harkness has observed, cannot be reduced to the contributions of any single participant.[16]

The foregoing discussion makes clear that most practitioners or scribes of theft magic never got in trouble with the law. As a result, we need to look more closely at those who did. The sampling of crimes in the Canterbury quarter session gaol delivery roll (Text 2.2) helps us position theft detection among comparable crimes dealt with by this court: petty heresy, theft, assault, and disorderly conduct. In short, it was a relatively minor crime, certainly not a felony. The presence of clerics among the accused in this selection of cases is unsurprising because their learning and religious offices made them attractive as cunning folk. Other practitioners were nonelite people who also had a modest level of learning, such as John Steward of Knaresburgh, who used the key-and-psalter method.[17] The operations performed by Thomas Barley and Nazareth Jarbrey (Text 2.3) were evidently drawn from the learned tradition of spirit conjuring exemplified in Text 2.14.

As was usual in prosecutions for magic in England prior to 1560, and as we see throughout this volume, many cases came to court because of the social disruption caused by the magician or their client rather than the magic itself. Of the five cases presented here, three are actually cases driven by the litigants' claim that they had been falsely accused or defamed (Texts 2.4, 2.5, and 2.6). That the false accusation was derived from magic no doubt made the case more likely to be of interest to officials, but magic was neither the litigant's nor the court's primary concern. Even the quarter session gaol delivery roll (Text 2.2) that identifies magic as Friar William's offense presents it as misbehavior rather than a grievous crime. He was *deceiving* the

---

16. Harkness, *John Dee's Conversations with Angels*, 11.

17. See Klaassen and Wright, *Magic of Rogues*, 108.

king's people. Returning to William Wycherly's claim, that there were hundreds of magic practitioners in England, the general disinclination to prosecute crimes of magic per se may well demonstrate that most magic practitioners never came to the attention of the courts simply because no one who knew about their activities objected to their work or was concerned enough to report it.

THE LEGAL TEXTS

Secular Courts

2.1. JOHN MOULD, DEFAMED THROUGH MAGICAL DETECTION, PETITIONS FOR HELP FROM CHANCERY (CA. 1467–72)[18]

To the right reverend Father in God and my right good and gracious lord the bishop of Bath and Wells, Chancellor of England, meekly beseecheth your poor orator John Mold, tilemaker; that whereas Peter Pemberton[19] of London, vintner, sent for your said orator, to the intent to have him to his servant, your said orator answered and said that he was in covenant with a yeoman of the king's house and might not serve him insomuch as he had made covenant afore with his master and so departed. And anon after that the said Pemberton sent for your said orator out of the country whereas he dwelleth, unto London to the place of the said Pemberton to the intent above said and your said orator answered and said as it is afore rehearsed. Whereupon the said Pemberton immediately to the intent to compel your said orator to do him service contrary to his first covenant, commenced an action of trespass against your said orator in London, surmising and saying that he should bear certain goods out of the house of the said Pemberton to the value of ten pounds. Also, the said Pemberton saith that he knoweth the very certainty thereof, for a man that looked in a glass by the craft of nigromancy told him diverse tokens that your said

18. Court of Chancery, Six Clerks Office. NA C/1/46/425. Written in English.

19. See "Peter Pemberton, Gentleman," in *Calendar of Plea and Memoranda Rolls, 1458–1482*, ed. Philip E. Jones (Cambridge: Cambridge University Press, 1961), 168.

orator should have the said goods, which craft by the law is damned. It is so, gracious Lord, that your said orator, by the means of his said master, would have found sufficient surety to answer to the said action according to the law. The said Pemberton understanding that, caused an alderman to lay his commandment upon[20] your said orator and in no wise will release him unless than your said orator will confess the said trespass by him done, or else to be covenant servant to the said Pemberton, which to do were against all right and good conscience and your said orator is likely to lie in prison to his uttermost undoing without your good and gracious Lordship to him be showed in this behalf. Please it therefore the same premises tenderly consider to grant a *corpus cum causa*[21] for your said orator direct to the Mayor and Sheriffs of London returnable at a certain day by your good lordship to be limited and your said orator shall specially pray [to] God for you.

Per Johanem Faukeswell

2.2. A CONJURING FRIAR AMONG OTHER OFFENDERS AT THE CANTERBURY COURT OF QUARTER SESSIONS
Gaol Delivery May 5, 1508[22]

The jury presents Christopher Banks, late of London, tailor, for heresy because he ate meat after Easter and was not shriven, nor were his rights taken.

Item: We present one friar William of the Black Friars [Dominicans] of the city of Canterbury for taking upon [himself] to conjure for men's goods to the great deceit of the king's people.

Item: We present the same Christopher Banks for stealing a dish from my lords of Canterbury, valued at 6 pence.

Item: We present Margett Benewyke for picking the purse of Shireland's wife.

20. = to put him in one of the London sheriffs' prisons, known as the counters

21. Aldermen could put people in the counters on suspicion of misdeeds for whatever term was deemed necessary. John Mold requests a writ of *corpus cum causa* in order to be released.

22. Canterbury Cathedral Archives and Library, CC/JQ/307/xiv fol. 20. Written in English.

Item: We present Catherine Dolfyn for suspicious rule keeping in her house.[23]

Item: We present the wife of one John Wattes for beating a poor woman.

Bishop of London's Courts

2.3. USE OF A BERYL STONE FOR CATCHING A THIEF[24]

St. Marie Abchurch [1476] Nazareth Jarbrey[25] on the 22nd day of February appeared before the commissary at the official's chambers, and after taking an oath to tell the truth she confessed that she was at Westminster with Thomas Barley in Tothill Street. After Thomas said certain prayers, she looked into a beryl stone, and the first time she saw in it a man in certain clothes, who carried a box[26] with pearls, stones and other things that had been stolen furtively from his mother's house. And again at the request of the cleric of the Church of St. George,[27] once more she went to the home of the same Thomas, and there similarly, she saw a man and a woman in certain clothes which she did not recognize, and after she described the dress and the appearance of the people, the cleric [of St. George] said that he knew the woman and she was named Longbele. And she [Nazareth] neither did nor said anything else. The case was carried over 8 days.[28]

23. The words "Bawedry keeping" were expunged.

24. LMA, DL/C/B/043/ MS09064/003 fol. 203r. Written in Latin. Hale, in *Precedents and Proceedings*, also transcribed the case (p. 10 no. 43) but thought Nazareth (a woman's name in this period) was a man and ignored the feminine pronouns in the manuscript.

25. A variant spelling of Garbry, a family name from Yarburgh, Lincolnshire (Gereburg in Domesday Book).

26. = unam pixidam. A pyx was most often used to hold a consecrated host, but well-to-do people could own them for private use. See, for example, the late medieval English pyx in the Victoria and Albert Museum, item number M.15&A-1950.

27. Probably St. George Botolph Lane, just to the east of Nazareth's parish of St. Marie Abchurch.

28. The court counted the current day, so eight days = one week.

2.4 MAGIC THEFT DETECTION[29]

St. Mary Axe [1497] Sir[30] Robert the rector is charged that he is a common defamer of many persons through his magic arts; and especially he defamed Alice Hall, saying that she furtively stole two rings of a certain Robert Draper, as set out through a bill written in his own hand; he has until next Saturday to respond to the articles.

2.5 PSALTER AND KEY[31]

St. Mary Magdalene [1497] John White is charged because in the parish of St. Mary Magdalene in Old Fish Street he employed the magic and prohibited art of psalter and key, by saying certain uses of the psalter. Through the said art he sought for one silver spoon from the goods of John Ryan; and through the said art he accused Elizabeth Doland as though [she were] guilty of the theft of the said spoon. Because of [White's] allegations Elizabeth's husband forced her from the house and from his fellowship and he beat her. The 26th of April the said John White appeared and confessed that he had been hired by the wife of John Ryan for 8 pence to look for the said stolen object with the psalter and key, by saying the verse "if you saw the thief"[32] and inserting the name of the said Elisabeth [into the key]. Because the key turned with the book with the said name, this John judged that the said Elisabeth was the culprit.

2.6 USE OF A MAGIC MIRROR[33]

St. Peter the Poor. [1502] Alice Anceyr is charged because she is a grave defamer of her neighbors and chiefly she defamed Christopher Sandon, saying that he carried off from her house a set of coral beads.[34]

---

29. LMA, DL/C/B/043/ MS09064/008 fol.100. Written in Latin. See also Hale, *Precedents and Proceedings*, 63 (no. 216).

30. = Dan. *Dan* was a shortened form for *dominus*. By the late fifteenth century it normally appeared in English as the title "Sir" for priests. It is akin to the term "Father" to designate a Catholic priest.

31. LMA, DL/C/B/043/ MS09064/008 fol. 58r. Written in Latin. Hale, *Precedents and Proceedings*, 61 (no. 207).

32. Psalm 49:18 Vulg.

33. LMA, DL/C/B/043/ MS09064/010 fol. 41r. Written in Latin. Hale, *Precedents and Proceedings*, 84 (no. 284).

34. Most likely a set of rosary beads, e.g., the coral beads in the list of items in the shop of Adam Ledyard, jeweler, of London, December 8, 1381, in Henry Thomas Riley, ed., *Memorials of London and London Life in the XIIIth, XIVth and XVth Centuries* ([S.l.]: Longmans, Green, 1868), 455.

Also, Alice was with a certain man staying in Charterhouse Street, who used the magical art. He reported to her, through the figure of his art, that he saw a picture and image of the aforesaid Christopher in a certain mirror; saying that this Christopher [while] standing at the glass window, observed Alice placing the set of beads in the straw of her bed, and after her departure, Christopher entered her room, and found the set of beads in the bed, which he took with him.

THE MAGIC TEXTS

2.7 THE EYE OF ABRAHAM[35]

For to find out a thief. Take the white of any hen's egg and *spuma argenti*,[36] that is for to say, the scum of silver that floats[37] above when it is melting, and wine, and mix[38] them together, and with that paint an eye on the wall this manner wise. ⬭⊃ And when thou hast painted the eye on the wall, say then this here following. [11v]

Glory to you, Lord God of our fathers. We acknowledge you, and we praise and bless you. We pray to you Lord that you deign to reveal the truth of this theft to us, just as Achor to your servant Joshua. And just as you revealed the truth concerning the two women to Solomon, you also showed the elders accusing Susanna to be false, and you turned aside [i.e., made manifest] the apostle Mathias in the election by lot,[39] in this way deign to reveal to us the truth of this theft and to show your omnipotence concerning what we seek, who are blessed for ever. Amen.[40]

So then in the presence before them all that thou hast in suspicion, and when he comes that is guilty, and if he looks on that eye that is painted on the wall his right eye will begin to water. And if it be so

35. Oxford, Bodleian Library, Additional B. 1., fol. 11r–11v.

36. Also known as litharge, lead oxide was a by-product of the smelting process and had been used since antiquity for various medical and cosmetic purposes.

37. *fleetes*

38. *minge*

39. This passage recalls several biblical stories in which the truth was revealed: Joshua 7:16–26; 1 Kings 3:16–28; Susanna 1. Mathias was chosen by lot to replace Judas as the twelfth apostle in Acts 1.

40. The entire prayer is written in Latin.

that thou ask him of that thing that is done away and he forsake[41] it, take then a skewer[42] or a nail of brass and set it rightly to the eye that is painted on the wall before him and smite on the nail with a hammer[43] and say thus:

"Rabbas seller Rabasasger."[44] And constrain that false thief for to yield and bring again what he has stolen and he shall smite his hand upon his eye and give a great cry.

2.8 THE BARLEYCORN METHOD[45]

Another knowledge for to bring out a thief. Take barleycorns and wash them in water that is called *aqua pensili[s]*.[46] And do them out of[47] the house under the sky and also [as] many men and women as [12r] thou hast suspected to set each one his name to his corn. And as thou namest the corns' names, let them fall into a vessel with water. That corn that draws toward the ground, he that is named after [it], is guilty, etc.

2.9. WAX IMAGES: "A PROVEN EXPERIMENT FOR MAKING A MALE OR FEMALE THIEF RETURN TO YOU IN PERSON IF HE SHOULD BE IN ANY PLACE WITHIN THE KINGDOM OF ENGLAND"[48]

First make two images of wax, that is, an image or a man and an image of a woman, and when they are done at the same time with both of them write in the front of the image "Yris" with this character ∇ and in the neck of the head "Sibilia" with this character ⌐⊔⌐ and in the top of of the head "Azaria" with this character o⌐ ⌐o. Then in the chest the name of the operator with these names Eleazar [and] Maligare, and this character ⌐ʄ⌐ and in the back opposite them this

41. = disavow
42. *broche*
43. *betell*
44. The words are meaningless.
45. Oxford, Bodleian Library, Additional B. 1., fols. 11v–12r.
46. Literally "hanging water," this may refer to a kind of hanging filtration system (*manicum hippocraticum*) used to create spiced wine. See John French, *The Art of Distillation, or, a Treatise* *of the Choicest Spagiricall Preparations Performed by Way of Distillation Together with the Description of the Chiefest Furnaces & Vessels Used by Ancient and Moderne Chymists* (London: Printed by E. Cotes, for Thomas Williams, 1653), 123–24.
47. *outwith*
48. Oxford, Bodleian Library, Additional B. 1., fols. 1r–2r. The entire ritual is in Latin.

character ⚹. Then make fire from dried whitethorn or from a thorn that is called eglantyne. Then take the aforesaid images, one in your hand and the other in the hand of your associate, and say this prayer:

God, founder and revealer of every invisible thing, to whom no secrets lie hidden, humbly we entreat your majesty that you deign to send Alexander Tebbe and Helen Tebbe, alias Dragis, to us in the strength of their crimes, yielded before us, that we may deserve to come to the worthy fatherland.[49] Amen.

[O] God, will you not revive us again that your people may rejoice in you?[50]

Let us pray.

Omnipotent and eternal God, founder and master of all things, disseminator of the virtue of all things from whom no secret lies hidden,[51] we humbly entreat that through the invocation of your holy names that you command your spirits Sabaoth, Uriel, and Ragnel to obey my injunctions that they make Alexander Tebbe and Elena Tebbe, alias Dragis, come back or turn back to me and confessing their crime so that we might be able to complete prayers of thanksgiving in your church.

Then take the two images to the fire but certainly take care that the wax not liquefy and then take both in your hand and say as follows.

"I conjure you Angels of God Sabaoth, Uriel, and Raguel, by the great potency of God the Father and the Son and the Holy Spirit, and by these names of God, which I invoke in my support: Ego sum Alpha et ω et primus et novissimus et Agla,[52] and by this name of God Tetragrammaton, and by this name of our Lord Jesus Christ at which every knee of celestial, terrestrial, and infernal beings is bent[53] and by the delights of heaven in which you are that in whatever country within the kingdom of England you compel Alexander Tebbe and

---

49. It seems likely the implication is "heaven" or "celestial fatherland."

50. Psalm 85:6. Also used in the Ordinary of the Latin Mass. See Francis Procter and Christopher Wordsworth, *Breviarium ad usum insignis ecclesiae sarum*, 3 vols. (Cambridge: Alma Mater Academia, 1879–86), 2:53, 153, and 239.

51. The Latin ("Deus cui omne cor patet . . .") seems to derive from the liturgy. See Francis Henry Dickinson, *Missale ad usum insignis et præclaræ ecclesiæ Sarum*, 4 vols. (Burntisland: E prelo de Pitsligo, 1861–83), 2:579.

52. = I am alpha and omega and first and most new and Agla

53. A common liturgical formula based upon Philippians 2:10–11.

Helen Tebbe to return to us by the virtue of these characters written in these images, and to return to us in all vigor, just as I fashion (them) in these images with this ring of thorn."[54]

And then prick the character with your needle.

"And that you not rest neither day nor night sitting, going, sleeping, or waking until they come to us. And let their heart flow on their arrival just as this wax of the image flowed from the face of the fire until they come to us and they confess their transgression."

Then keep both images without damage in a box in clean cloths; since if they are damaged in some place that person will be destroyed. Know for certain that this experiment is true and approved and without any danger to soul or body since it is done by three angels, Sabaoth, Uriel, and Raguel.

End of this experiment.

2.10. EXPERIMENTS TO FIND THIEVES (INCLUDING CIPHERS)[55]

When you go to bed put the words following, being written in virgin wax,[56] under your head before you go to bed: agios + agios + spratus + sacoiro famulo nuo. Probatum.[57]

Aliter[58] (a7wt9r)

Write these words in virgin wax with olive oil:[59]

$$\not\equiv \cdot \mathcal{B} \cdot \not\equiv \cdot \text{\textcrb} \cdot \not\equiv \cdot \mathcal{B} \cdot \not\equiv$$

And lay it under thy head when thou goest to bed and thou shalt see he that stole thy goods in thy sleep. Et fiat.[60]

---

54. The Latin text could read "with a ring of spit" but is not clear.

55. London, British Library, Sloane 3850, fols. 16or–61r.

56. This is to say, wax that has never been used for anything else.

57. Despite meaning proven or tested, it is very unlikely the scribe tried it. Instead, this is a way of lending the text the appearance of authority. The preceding four words are meaningless. Claire Jones, "Formula and Formulation: 'Efficacy Phrases,'" *Neuphilologische Mittelungen* 99, no. 2 (1998): 199–209.

58. = Another (for the same purpose)

59. *oyle vlyfe*

60. Translatable as "and let it be done," this phrase has several layers of meaning. It is an "efficacy phrase" like *probatum*, implying that the effect desired will be accomplished. It also echoes words from the Latin Vulgate with which God spoke the world into being: "*Fiat lux* (Let there be light)." It is also the standard translation of the Hebrew word *amen*.

Pro furto[61]
Write these letters in virgin wax with olive oil: . o . b . o . t . b . r . Lay it under thy head and then go to bed and you shall see he that stole thy goods. Et fiat.

To find a thief
Take a dagger and lay it in a psalter by the psalm "Whomsoever will be saved, etc."[62] And shut the book closed and write the names of as many as you do suspect upon some dry pieces of paper and lay them by the dagger. Then take another psalter and read the psalm aforesaid two or three times over, and if any of them whose names be written stole the goods, the psalter will dance and his name will leap and lie on top,[63] and if he be not amongst the names, then it will not stir. Et fiat. Probatum.

Another
Take quicksilver and mingle it with the white of and egg and draw[64] a man's eye with it on a wall and call in all them you suspect and bid them behold the same eye well. And then his eye will water that is guilty and if he or she confesses not, take a nail and prick the eye that is pictured and cry, "Ye hares!"[65] And the party that is guilty will cry, "*veh oculum!*"[66] Let it be done.

To see a thief in the night
Take and write these names in thy left hand: O Agios, O Spirit, let you be as a servant.[67] Amen. And when thou goest to sleep, lay thy hand on thy knee and thou shalt dream of him that stole thy goods. Fiat. Probatum. [161r]

---

61. = For theft
62. Psalm 80:3 or 80:7.
63. *overmoste*
64. *picttore*
65. It is not clear if the meaning is rabbits, the archaic word for a group of people (here), or whores.

66. = Oh, [my] eye
67. The Latin optimistically reads, "O Agios, O Spiritus, sit tam famulo. Amen."

If a man have stolen any thing, touch him with the herb vervain under the breast and he will confess it. Et fiat. And also if one bear it about him, none shall have power over him of his enemies to hurt him. Et fiat. Probatum.

To know him that have stolen anything.

Write these names in virgin wax when the sun is in Leo or in Gemini: "Aga: thief: alphia: gos: Desertum.[68]" And lay it under thy head when thou goest to bed and thou shall see him that stole thy goods in thy sleep. Probatum.

2.11. KEY AND PSALTER VERSION ONE[69]

Experiment with a book and key for revealing a thief through the names of the suspected. But see that when you wish to operate that you should be clean in conscience and constant in the Catholic faith.

"Sel, Alliel, Echel, Agla, et Ely Panton, I conjure you. Craton rex Jesus Nazarenus etc.[70] Let the name of the Lord be blessed etc."[71]

Prayer.

"We beseech you, Lord, by inspiring to lead our actions and by commanding to attend to them, so that our every prayer and work begins from you and what was begun is brought to an end in you. Amen."[72]

"Lord Jesus Christ, who scrutinizes the loins and hearts of men,[73] Lord God who said, I alone know all things, I am the living bread which descended from heaven,[74] Lord who is alpha and omega, first and

68. *Desertum* may mean "desert" or "deserted."

69. London, British Library, Sloane 3846, 81v–83r. All is in Latin except paragraph beginning "then take a psalter."

70. The syntax is peculiar. "Etc." indicates that this is the beginning of a passage known to the writer. It seems likely upon the power of divine names rather than a adjuration of Jesus.

71. A liturgical usage. See W. H. Frere, *The Use of Sarum*, 2 vols. (Cambridge: University Press, 1898), 2:72 and 90.

72. This prayer originates in the Catholic liturgy. Robert Lippe and H. A. Wilson, *Missale Romanum Mediolani, 1474*, 2 vols., Henry Bradshaw Society 17, 33 (London: [Printed for the Society by Harrison and Sons], 1899–1907), 2:115 and 117. For one of many examples of its use in magic, see Gösta Hedegård, ed., *Liber Iuratus Honorii—A Critical Edition of the Latin Version of the Sworn Book of Honorius* (Stockholm: Almqvist & Wiksell International, 2002), 72 (VI).

73. Psalm 7:10.

74. John 6:41.

most new, through your most holy name which is Tetragrammaton, and through the miracles, [82r] merits, and intercessions of Peter and Paul although we are sinners, we beg of your mercy, that if the person whose name was written on this paper is the culprit in this deed, that you will deign to demonstrate to us in the virtue of God by the turning the book and key, and if he is not the culprit, it not be moved, neither book nor key, so that you deign to reveal the culprit in this deed through the inseparable Trinity, Father, Son, and Holy Spirit, and as you satiated the four thousand people with four loaves of bread and two fishes, so deign to show us the full and perfect truth in this matter, through Christ our Lord. Amen."

Then take a psalter book and put in a key upon this verse, fast clasped, and hold it steadfast upon your foremost fingers without shaking, and put with the key into the book the name of the suspected [person], and it will turn if he be guilty, if he be not, it will not turn.

"In the name of the Father, and of the Son, and of the Holy Spirit. Amen. I adjure you, book, by God the Father, Son, and Holy Spirit, and by holy Mary, mother of our lord Jesus Christ, and by holy Michael, archangel, and by all the holy angels and archangels, by thrones, dominations, principalities, and powers, and by all the virtues of the heavens, [82v] and by patriarchs and prophets, and by the holy apostle Peter, and Paul and Andreas, and by all the other holy apostles and evangelists of God, and by the forty-four thousand innocents, and by the holy Stephan, protomartyr, and by all the holy martyrs of God, and by the holy confessor Nicholas, and by all the confessors of God, and by holy Mary Magdalene and by Mary of Egypt,[75] and by every male and female saint of God. I adjure you, book, by these holy names of God, Jesus, Sanctus, Salvator, Alpha et Omega, Adonay, Emanuel, On, the holy ineffable name, by all of these names, and by the seven gifts of the Holy Spirit, and by all the bishops and archbishops, priests, deacons, subdeacons, and every rank of the church, and by the masses which are sung within her, and by the holy body of Christ that was sacrificed. I adjure you by paradise and by all the mansions of paradise and by all things that are in in paradise.

75. Patron saint of penitents
(ca. 344–ca. 421).

I adjure you, book, by the world and everything that is in the world, by fire and by all things that are in fire, by air and by everything that is in air, and by the sun and the moon, and by every heavenly body, by water and by all things that are in water, by earth and by all things that are in the earth, and by every virtue of god and his works, that if this .N. is the culprit of this crime, you should turn in a gyre, just as the sun turns on its pivot point."

"Give to the king thy judgment."

"Have mercy on me, O God."

"Our Father."[76]

These should be said three times, the conjuration as well.

2.12 KEY AND PSALTER VERSION TWO[77]

To know a thief. Proven.

Write the name of him whom you suspect and hide the writing in the hole of a key.[78] Then let the key be suspended from the hands of two people. [Say] "When you saw a thief, you ran with him; and with adulterers you have been a partaker."[79] And you will see the key and book at once move.

Do it in this way.

<hr />

76. These three phrases (in Latin) are the first lines of things to be recited by memory: Psalm 71 Vulg.; Psalm 50 Vulg.; the Lord's Prayer.

77. London, British Library, Sloane 3318, fol. 102r. Latin.

78. I.e., in the hollow stem.

79. *Cum videbis furem currebas cum illo et cum adultores portionem tuam ponebas.* Psalm 49:18 Vulg. Translation from Douay-Reims 1899.

2.13. CLAY BALLS TECHNIQUE[80]

To find out anything that is lost
Write the names of every person suspected by himself [i.e., individually] in parchment, and wrap every one by himself in clay. He or she that did the fact shall swim and then fall in [i.e., float and sink].

But before you put them into the water first say: "Glory be to thee, O Father. We laud, pray, and magnify thee, O Lord of our father Abraham, Isaac, and Jacob. We beseech thee that thou wilt vouchsafe to show us the truth of this deed, as thou didst show the deed of Achan to Joshua, and hast revealed to Solomon the 2 harlots, and has showed, and has showed Matthew thy apostle the election, and hast judged by Daniel the two priests falsely accusing Susanna, so truly show to us, our Lord, who is the author of this treason or fact committed whom we now seek with art, blessed for ever & ever world without end. Amen."

Say this three times and then three Pater Nosters, one Ave Maria, and one Creed. But say it not on the first day of any month nor the 2nd, 4th, nor 5th, 6th, 7th, 9th, 11th, 13th, 15th for those days are evil for that purpose.

2.14. SCRYING FOR THIEVES IN A STONE[81]

Experimentum
To the finding of theft or of the state of friends or of treasures hidden or not hidden or of other things whatsoever they be in the world.

You shall first [have] a child lawfully born with twelve years of age and a great crystal stone or beryl, whole and sound.[82] And let it be anointed with olive oil hallowed and then the child shall say after the master three times: "Andromalce,[83] come thou with haste and that I may perceive thee with my sight and other things."

80. London, British Library, Sloane 3846, fol. 71v.

81. London, British Library, Sloane 3849, fol. 17r–18r. For an earlier Latin version, see Oxford, Bodleian Library, Rawlinson D. 252, fol. 119r–119v.

82. "Lawfully born" means born in wedlock. On the use of a virgin child in magic, see Claire Fanger, "Virgin

Territory: Purity and Divine Knowledge in Late Medieval Catoptromantic Texts," *Aries* 5, no. 2 (2005): 200–25.

83. Adromalcus appears in numerous manuscripts in connection with necromantic rituals. See Oxford, Bodleian Library, Rawlinson D. 252, 119r and 144r; London, British Library, Sloane 3825, fol. 126; 3829, fol. 17; 3846,

Then say "*Benedicte dominus. In nomine patris et filii* etc."[84] But first consecrate the oil [in] this manner.

"I conjure thee oil by the holy baptism of God and by [the] same holy ointment that the three Marys did bear to the sepulcher that they might anoint the body of Christ buried.[85] In like manner be thou holding [and] receiving such virtue that, from [the spirits'] entrance into this stone, the compass of which shall be anointed, they shall not have power to hide the truth, but [rather] of showing openly of all things that I shall ask him or them to be inquired of.

"*In nomine patris* etc."

"[I] conjure thee Andromalcus by our Lord the Father omnipotent, by the true God, by the holy God, by the God which did cast thee from the joys of paradise and by these names of God, Messias, Emanuel, Otheos, Athanathos, Eli, Panton, Craton, and Ysus, Alpha and Omega, Jesus Nazarenus Christus, On, El and by all the names of Christ and of God. I do conjure thee, Andromalcus, by Tetragrammaton, Horoiall, Heomaldall, Abhoalfanal, Agla, Lamazabetham, Engoni, Regon, Gramaton, Spirem, Emirison. And by Holy Mary, the mother of our Lord Jesus Christ, and by the five joys of her, and by the virginity of John the Evangelist, and by these names, Mapoth, Napoth, by which Solomon did close you in a vessel of glass that whereso- [17v] ever you shalt be now, you shall, by and by, enter to this crystal stone or into this glass or stone glass to the sight of this child and me in fair form of mankind, having color red or white, without any fear or hurt of me or this child or any other being in this company and without grievance of body and soul. Amen."

And then the master shall say devoutly the psalm, *Deus in nomine tuo* etc.[86] And then ask the child if he sees anything. And if no, let the master begin his conjuration again until he do come to the second "I conjure thee." Then let the child say after the master three times, "Andromalcus come" etc. This done, the master shall say on[c]e:

"I command the by the virtue of the living God, true and purer and most merciful, and by that same angel the which doth sing in a

fol. 83v. K. M. Briggs, *The Anatomy of Puck: An Examination of Fairy Beliefs Among Shakespeare's Contemporaries and Successors* (London: Routledge & Kegan Paul, 1959), 255–61.

84. The liturgical source is unclear.
85. Mark 16:1–8. See also Matthew 28:1–9; Luke 23:55; John 21:1.
86. Psalm 53 Vulg.

tube [i.e., sound the trumpet][87] in the day of judgment and shall say, "Come ye blessed,"[88] and by angels and archangels, thrones, dominations, principates, powers, cherubim, and seraphim, and by all relics of men saints and women saints of God the which be contained in the world, and as Mary was a true virgin in her birth and before and after, and as it is true that the host, the which was bred, is converted into the flesh of our Lord Jesus Christ, and by the names by which be the greatest in necromancy, Balsake super balsorke panulo in the power part aye saryae serpasys,[89] to the which names waters be stayed and the elements be stricken, and by these names, I command thee by the charity of God and by the eyes of him, and by all members of him and by the deity of him and by the good and evil by which the elements doth suffer of them.

"I do conjure thee that thou shall sit, or thee shall sit, before me [18r] and this child in declaring and showing to all [of us] our answers and questions, and in writing, that it [being] written may be to our understanding and full answer and satisfying to our will and mind."

And then ask what thou wilt and thou shall have an answer and this secret ought not to be shown [to anyone] as thou art wise. And when thou shall be certified of your mind, give to him this license saying:

"I do conjure thee, Andromalcus[90] or thou, by all the names afore rehearsed that thou dost go to the place thee came from and whensoever I shall call thou or any of thou, be thee ready always to me, and when I call upon thou and the peace of God, let it be between us and thou. *In nomine patris* etc."

And let the master say over the child's head and he shall not be hurt nor any other being in his company and about him.

Sequence of the Holy Gospel According to John. Glory to you etc. In the beginning was the Word and the Word was with God etc.[91]

<hr/>

87. Evidently a mistranslation of *in tuba dei canet* from the Latin version. See Oxford, Bodleian Library, Rawlinson D. 252, fol. 119v.

88. Thessalonians 4:16.

89. This is an mix of translated Latin and fanciful divine names. The earlier Latin version is clearly related: "Balsas Superbalsat. barri. molum potestate hay Saristie sede cerperis." Oxford,

Bodleian Library, Rawlinson D. 253, fol. 17v.

90. The scribe here writes Andrewmalcus rather than Andromalcus.

91. John 1. The sequences were a part of the liturgy, in the case the first chapter of John. This was preceded in the liturgy by the phrase *Gloria tibi, Domine* (Glory to you, Lord).

CHAPTER 3

Love Magic

Love magic presents the historian with a thorny set of interpretive problems. Bad love magic was almost uniformly associated with women in the premodern period, and men certainly projected their fears of women's sexual power over them onto it. Any case of love magic must be read through this lens, but modern historians' attention to this projection and the othering of women, notably in celebrity cases, gives us a partial and potentially misleading picture in several ways. Women and men practiced different kinds of love magic, but there is no evidence that women practiced it more often. Moreover, if surviving manuscripts are any indication, premodern love magic included a broad range of goals in addition to provoking erotic or amorous feelings, including promoting or preventing conception, assessing a woman's chastity or loyalty, discovering or determining the sex of a child, currying favor, or enlivening a marriage. The texts may also have served as a fantasy, as much as literary works such as *A Midsummer Night's Dream* or *Tristan and Isolde*. Finally, accusations of performing love magic for women could be a way to denigrate a male practitioner. An accurate understanding of love magic has to balance all of these elements.

A number of celebrity cases reflect not only fear of women's sexual power over men but also women's disempowerment.[1] Well known, for example, is the case of Eleanor, Duchess of Gloucester, whose husband, Humphrey, was a potential heir to the childless Henry VI. Eleanor was convicted and imprisoned for treasonable necromancy in 1441. Part of the evidence against her was her association with the cunning

---

1. See also the earlier case of Alice Perrers, mistress of Edward III, who was reputed to have employed love magic. W. Mark Ormrod, "The Trials of Alice Perrers," *Speculum* 83, no. 2 (2008): 366–96; E. M. Thompson, ed., *Chronicon Angliae* (London: Longman, 1874), 98–100.

woman Marjory Jourdemayne, the "Witch of Eye," who provided the barren duchess with recipes for conception.[2] Another well-known example is Richard III's 1483 accusation of Edward IV's widow, Elizabeth Woodville, and her mother, Jaquetta of Luxembourg, of using sorcery to secure Elizabeth's marriage to the king.[3] Finally, in 1533 the Savoyard diplomat and Catholic priest Eustace Chapuys complained that Anne Boleyn had so enchanted and bewitched Henry VIII that he would do nothing against her will.[4] Shortly after Anne's miscarriage in 1536, Chapuys also recorded circulating rumors that the king blamed his lack of a male heir on a marriage made through sortilege.[5] These highly politicized cases reveal gendered fears about the connection between love magic, women's complicated sexual power over men, and the perceived threat to social order. They also highlight how women were disempowered in marriage negotiations and held responsible for producing a male heir, a matter out of their control. In both circumstances, women might well have turned to magic, which is in large measure focused on controlling the uncontrollable. In the ancient world, women's love magic tended to focus on securing or preserving marriages, a pattern we see here and below.[6] However, these give only a partial picture of the actual practice of love magic.

2. G. L. Harriss, "Eleanor [née Eleanor Cobham], Duchess of Gloucester (c. 1400–1452), Alleged Sorcerer," in *Oxford Dictionary of National Biography* (Oxford: Oxford University Press, 2008), https://doi.org/10.1093/ref:odnb/5742. Jessica Freeman, "Sorcery at Court and Manor: Margery Jourdemayne, the Witch of Eye Next Westminster," *Journal of Medieval History* 30, no. 4 (2004): 343–57. See also Young, *Magic as a Political Crime*, 35–45.

3. Great Britain, Parliament, *Rotuli Parliamentorum; ut et petitiones, et placita in Parliamento tempore Edwardi R. I. [ad finem Henrici VII.]*, vol. 6, p. 251. See also Young, *Magic as a Political Crime*, 47–48; H. A. Kelly, "English Kings and the Fear of Sorcery," *Medieaval Studies* 39 (1977): 235.

4. "Spain: 16 December 1533," in *Calendar of State Papers, Spain*, vol. 4, part 2, *1531–1533*, ed. Pascual de Gayangos (London: Her Majesty's Stationery Office, 1882), 880–95. *British History Online*, https://www.british-history.ac.uk/cal-state-papers/spain/vol4/no2/pp880-895.

5. "Spain: 29 January 1536," in *CSP, Spain*, vol. 5, part 2, *1536–1538*, ed. Pascual de Gayangos (London: Her Majesty's Stationery Office, 1888), 11–29. *British History Online*, https://www.british-history.ac.uk/cal-state-papers/spain/vol5/no2/pp11-29.

6. Christopher A. Faraone, *Ancient Greek Love Magic* (Cambridge, MA: Harvard University Press, 1999), 96–131.

The inclination among premodern people (as well as some modern historians) to regard love magic as a peculiarly female activity is not supported by English evidence.[7] Magic manuscripts were written almost uniformly by men (e.g., Text 3.6) and contain significant amounts of love magic.[8] Naturally, one cannot assume scribes practiced the magic they wrote down. However, legal evidence suggests that purveyors of love magic were just as frequently male as female and that they served clients of both sexes and in roughly equal numbers. This is also attested in preaching and pastoral literature.[9] Evidence from the continent, especially southern Europe, suggests that a significant number of women, often accused of working in the sex trade, ended up in court for using love magic.[10] This could be taken as a confirmation of the association of women with love magic (like the celebrity cases above). At the same time, it is difficult to disentangle the accusations of magic from the charged social roles played by prostitutes in order to determine if they actually practiced the art. In fact, as we shall see, what brought love magic into the courts was less the magic itself than issues of fraud, sexual misbehavior, and social disruption, or all of these combined.

The 1482 case of Joan Beverly (Text 3.2) in the bishop of London's courts illustrates why we must take care in interpreting accusations of love magic in cases involving social disruption or threats to patriarchal

7. See Maxwell-Stuart, *British Witch*, 114. A similar claim is made by Robin Briggs, *Witches and Neighbours: The Social and Cultural Context of European Witchcraft* (London: Harper-Collins, 1996), 321. For men outnumbering women, see David Gentilcore, *From Bishop to Witch: The System of the Sacred in Early Modern Terra d'Otranto* (Manchester: Manchester University Press, 1992), 23; Kevin C. Robbins, "Magical Emasculation, Popular Anticlericalism, and the Limits of the Reformation in Western France Circa 1590," *Journal of Social History* 31 (1997): 66–67.

8. Richard Kieckhefer, "Erotic Magic in Medieval Europe," in *Sex in*

the Middle Ages: A Book of Essays, ed. Joyce E. Salisbury (New York: Garland, 1991), 30–55.

9. Late medieval pastoral manuals paint a similar picture. See Catherine Rider, "Women, Men, and Love Magic in Late Medieval English Pastoral Manuals," *Magic, Ritual, and Witchcraft* 7, no. 2 (2012): 208. For other, see Macfarlane, *Witchcraft in Tudor and Stuart England*, 121.

10. See Mary O'Neil, "Magical Healing, Love Magic and the Inquisition in Late Sixteenth-Century Modena," in *Inquisition and Society in Early Modern Europe*, ed. and trans. Stephen Haliczer (London: Croom Helm, 1987), 89–101.

control. The record describes Joan as a "bawd"—that is, as a procurer of prostitutes—and mentions a network of relationships involving multiple men, including Joan's husband. Gentlemen fought over her, sometimes almost to the death, and her husband left her for fear of being assaulted or killed. Joan was also described as living with another bawd. From the case it seems that the accusation of love magic is secondary to the problem of sexual and social disorder. Indeed, we cannot be sure Joan actually practiced love magic. It seems just as credible that the men involved in this public scandal tried to explain their misbehavior by claiming they were enchanted. Seen in this light, accusations of love magic performed by women were a way of accounting for men's failures or shortcomings. This was certainly the case surrounding concerns that impotence might be magically induced.[11]

In Text 3.1, Mariot de Belton and Isabella Brome appeared before the church courts described as *sortilegae* who used love magic. The accused women may have been genuine cunning women, possibly even specialists of love magic who helped women secure men for marriage. This follows patterns mentioned above. It might also be the case that the charges against Mariot and Isabella were entirely trumped up and that desiring and manipulating men was the only thing their defaming accusers could imagine women wanting to do. This entry (like the case of Joan Beverly) illustrates how difficult it can be to evaluate the magic practices of women through legal sources that often give far less detail in cases of women than of men. Mariot and Isabella's case is so short that it would be difficult to say whether the real issue was the potential breach of canon law around marriage consent more than the magic.

In the case of Margaret Williamson (Text 3.4), the court seems to have been less concerned with her use of a love potion (a single incident) than with her ownership of a suspect book, presumably a book of magic. This suggests that she was engaged not only with learned traditions of magic but also its informal networks of transmission, both usually associated with men.[12] The mention of the book reminds

---

11. On witchcraft and impotence, see Catherine Rider, *Magic and Impotence in the Middle Ages* (Oxford: Oxford University Press, 2006), 188–207.

12. Klaassen and Wright, *Magic of Rogues*, 16 and 143.

us that, as with female medical practitioners, we cannot assume that a female magician employed only popular or nonliterate traditions.

Cases involving male practitioners of love magic are often much more detailed. They do not normally display the same level of focus on the magical practitioner's sexual misbehavior, although, as we have suggested in the case of Robert Allen, associating a man with love magic and women's activities might have been a way of denigrating him. Also, as in cases involving female practitioners, it is not always clear that magic, much less love magic, was the main concern for the prosecuting officials. For example, fraud and social disharmony feature prominently in the cases of Richard Laukiston (Text 3.3) and Thomas Fansome (Text 3.5). Laukiston confessed to acting as a middleman between a poor widow, Margaret Geffrey, and an unnamed cunning man who would procure her a husband.

The case of Thomas Fansome (Text 3.5) provides some useful perspectives on the extent to which men were involved in both the performance and use of love magic. He confessed to multiple instances of taking payment for love and sex magic, which seems to have been his particular specialty in addition to healing. The fact that he names as many male as female clients suggests men sought such magic as often as women. Nor were male providers and consumers of love magic unusual. In 1561 John Devon, alias Coxe, confessed to involvement in love magic performed by a man called Bisson to provoke the love of the widow of Richard Cotton.[13] Simon Forman wrote about love magic and was consulted on matters of love. Finally, the cunning man Robert Allen (Text 1.1) was reputed to have performed love magic.[14] The common assumption that love magic was a peculiarly female affair is thus not sustainable. This is suggested even more strongly in the manuscripts.

Most premodern manuscripts were written by and for men, and magic manuscripts were no different. These quite frequently contain

13. *State Papers Online, 1509–1714, Pt. 1, The Tudors, Henry VIII to Elizabeth I, 1509–1603, State Papers Domestic* (Gale Cengage Learning, 2016), SP 12/16 Sequence Number 120 and 125.

14. A. L. Rowse, *Sex and Society in Shakespeare's Age: Simon Forman the Astrologer* (New York: Scribner, 1974), 257; Lauren Kassell, *Medicine and Magic in Elizabethan London: Simon Forman, Astrologer, Alchemist, and Physician*, Oxford Historical Monographs (Oxford: Clarendon Press, 2005), 77 and 232. On Robert Allen, see chapter 1 above.

love magic, a good deal of which was focused purely on sex. At first glance, this seems to confirm common assumptions about male versus female love magic: in general, that women used it to establish or preserve marriage and men to compel others to have sex with them.[15] As Christopher Faraone has argued, these reveal a view of sexuality opposite to the usual premodern construction of women as sexually voracious.[16] The legal texts 3.1, 3.3, and 3.5 all fall into this pattern, as do most of the examples of love magic in manuscript. However, a second look at the manuscripts reveals a greater level of commonality between the sexes. Male scribes of magic manuscripts commonly included goals other than sex in the sections they dedicated to love magic. These include operations for provoking romantic love in women *or* men, for stirring love in a spouse of either sex, promoting or preventing conception, choosing the sex of a child, overcoming sexual dysfunction, and determining whether a woman was a virgin or a loyal wife. Finally, magic to attain the love or goodwill of social superiors (usually by a man and focused on another man) also appears in the same mix.

The book "Of Love, of Kardes, Dies and Tables, and Other Consaytes," from which Text 3.6 was drawn, exemplifies this pattern. The collection contains a wide variety of operations for love together with sections on gambling, hunting, and fishing (see Texts 4.4–4.6). One of these describes how not only to get a ring of invisibility from a beautiful spirit (clearly a fairy) but also to have sex with her![17] As a whole, the collection is suggestive of the adolescent and rakish interests of young men like Harry Neville (Text 4.1) and may have served as much as an entertainment as a practical magic sourcebook. Certainly, the section on love magic focuses on erotic magic. However, it also includes many other forms of love magic that were intended to be used within or in support of marriages or conventional social relations. For example, it also contains less obviously male-focused magic such as assessing whether a "womb is corrupted" or promoting

---

15. Rider, "Women, Men, and Love Magic," 208.

16. Faraone, *Ancient Greek Love Magic*.

17. See Frank Klaassen and Katrina Bens, "Achieving Invisibility and Having Sex with Spirits: Six Operations from an English Magic Collection, ca. 1600," *Opuscula* 3, no. 1 (2013): 1–14.

conception of children. That some of these were explicitly intended to be performed on behalf of women confirms the pattern seen in the Fansome and Laukiston cases (Texts 3.3 and 3.5), where women hired men to perform love magic.

Taken together, the manuscripts and court cases pose an interesting problem. In principle, almost any kind of love magic was threatening and potentially destabilizing to a patriarchal society. Men employed claims of love magic to exculpate their own failures, and they suspected women of performing it to subvert patriarchal privilege and authority. Magic manuscripts, largely written for men, attempted to procure other men's wives, daughters, or sisters, subverting male control over female family members. Divination regarding fertility, chastity, or fidelity might also result in slanderous accusations. Magic to induce favor from a male superior also subverted the established patriarchal order. Finally, it is clear that love magic was relatively commonplace. It appears often and in significant quantities in magic manuscripts, as Text 3.6 illustrates. The case of Thomas Fansome (Text 3.5) makes clear that there was an active market for love magic and that both men and women used it. So it is a curious matter that, as David Cressy has argued, clear cases of love magic in Tudor England are so hard to find,[18] unlike the cases of magic for identifying thieves. The love magic cases presented here are among the very few found in English courts. The reasons for this are far from clear, but let us make a few suggestions.

Cunning folk would have had good reason to be cautious with love magic and may well have avoided it, at least in some of its forms. Magic for detecting thieves, for luck in gambling, hunting, or fishing, for healing or protection, for finding treasure, or for forcing demons into service (in principle at least) had no innocent victim: one did not sympathize with a thief, other gamblers, animals, or demons. Love magic, by contrast, manipulated an unconscious human subject and potentially disrupted marriages or their negotiation. Cunning folk were typically regarded with respect and guarded their reputations

18. David Cressy, *Birth, Marriage, and Death: Ritual, Religion, and the Life-Cycle in Tudor and Stuart England* (Oxford: Oxford University Press, 1997), 265. On the continent they appear to be more frequent. See O'Neil, "Magical Healing," 89–101.

carefully. They would have had every reason to avoid performing magic that was potentially disruptive. On the other hand, a good deal of love magic was not a threat to social order. At very least, ensuring that a wife was faithful, that a potential spouse was a virgin, that a husband loved his wife, and that a couple had children all sought to *reinforce* conventional marriages and gendered hierarchies.

Moreover, as we find with magic in general, many of the cases of love magic are known not because of the magic but because of other more serious accusations to which the practice of love magic was merely additional evidence. John Devon, cited above, came to the attention of the ecclesiastical authorities for performing Catholic Masses and love magic. Robert Allen (chapter 1) was imprisoned for predicting the death of the king and was reported to have performed love magic. Thomas Fansome was referred to only as a "counterfayte physytion," and the paper hung about his neck in the stocks read, "A longe ffornicator, A lewde charmer, A counterfayte physytion" despite the fact that (if his confession is any indication) love magic was his specialty. The court evidently gave equal weight to his being a false physician and fornicator as it did to his charming.[19] There is also no evidence that it was the love magic that brought him to the attention of the authorities. The fact that he claimed to have learned physic as a physician's servant and made a great production about his positive testimonial letters suggests that his medical activities were the court's central concern. Outside of London, the regulation and licensing of physicians was the responsibility of the bishops, and this case gives every indication of being focused primarily on his unlicensed practice. Calling him a "lewd" (i.e., unlearned) charmer may have been intended principally to indicate that he was an unfit medical practitioner rather than to indicate a separate crime.[20]

19. Unlicensed practitioners were regulated through excommunication. For example, William Bateman from Suffolk was excommunicated in 1597 for practicing surgery without a license. J. F. Williams, ed., *Diocese of Norwich, Bishop Redman's Visitation, 1597: Presentments in the Archdeaconries of* *Norwich, Norfolk, and Suffolk*, Norfolk Record Society 18 ([Norfolk]: Norfolk Record Society, 1946), 134.

20. Curiously, a Thomas Fansham was given a license to operate as a surgeon in diocese of Canterbury on March 14, 1590. See Lambeth Palace Library Whitgift 1, fol. 163v.

The courts, following their practical nature, may also have excluded some cases of love magic, such as claims that a marriage had been procured through magic. It cannot be coincidental that we have yet to find a single example in matrimonial causes in which a marriage is disputed on the grounds of love magic, even the celebrity cases we mentioned at the start of the chapter. In the absence of other incriminating evidence, such a case would be hard to bring, particularly since the burden of proof lay upon the litigant and also because canon lawyers would gravitate toward concrete evidence. Discovering whether consent had been given and consummation performed was much easier than discovering magical inducement of those actions. The social disruption of fractured marriages (or false marriages, as in the case of the Fansomes) was of far greater concern to the ecclesiastical authorities than the happiness of the couple. Unlike theft detection, which commonly found its way into the courts because someone had been defamed falsely, love magic did not have any such indisputable victims unless someone confessed to doing it.

THE LEGAL TEXTS

3.1. MAGICALLY PROCURING HUSBANDS FOR SINGLE WOMEN[21]

October 1446. Mariot de Belton and Isabella Brom. It is imputed that [Mariot] is a witch[22] and that she uses that art, and that she said to unmarried women who desired to marry that she will make them have whom they want and desire. She denies this and has to purge herself twelve-handed.[23] The same is imputed to Isabella. She denies this and has to purge herself four-handed.

21. Durham Cathedral Archive (DCD), Cap. Prior fol. 62r. Written in Latin. See also James Raine, ed., *Depositions and Other Ecclesiastical Proceedings from the Courts of Durham*, Surtees Society (London: J. B. Nichols and Son, 1845), 29. See also Davies, *Cunning-Folk*, 2.

22. *sortilega*.

23. I.e., she must come back to court with twelve people who will swear to her good character.

3.2. MAGIC TO SEDUCE MEN[24]

St. Sepulcher Without Newgate [1482] Joan Beverly at Lessell near Cowcross [Street] is a witch[25] and she convinced 2 kindred witches that they should bring it about that Robert Stanton and another gentleman of Gray's Inn would desire her and no other. And these men committed adultery with her and, as it is said, these men fought for her, and one nearly killed the other, and her husband dared not remain with her on account of these 2 men, and she is a common whore, and a bawd, and wants to poison men, because her art has failed. And Agnes dwelling with her is a bawd.

3.3. TAKING ADVANTAGE OF A WIDOW WITH THE PROMISE OF LOVE MAGIC[26]

St. Mary Magdalene. Because of public fame circulating, our official investigated a certain Richard Laukiston from the parish of St. Mary Magdalene in Old Fish Street, and Margaret Geffrey a widow recently from the parish of St. Bartholomew the Less, concerning and upon certain articles touching the crime of heresy and sorcery; namely, that Richard in AD 1480[27] in the months of January, February, March, and April or in any of the aforementioned months, namely that Richard uttered these words or [words] similar to them to the aforesaid Margaret in English: "You are a poor widow, and it is an act of charity to help you to marry, and if you will do any expense in spending money, you shall have a man worth a thousand pounds." Then the widow Margaret answered: "How may that be?" Then Laukiston said, "My wife knoweth a cunning man, that by his cunning can cause a woman to have any man that she hath favor to, and that will be guaranteed,[27] for she hath put it in execution afore time, and this shall cost money." Then Margaret said, "I have no goods save 2 mazers for to fund me, my mother, and my children, and if they were sold and I fail of my purpose, I, my

24. London, Metropolitan Archives (LMA), DL/C/B/043/MS09064/003 fol. 115r. Written in Latin. See also Hale, *Precedents and Proceedings*, 7 (no. 27).

25. LMA, DL/C/B/043/ MS09064/005 fols. 29v, 30r. Written mainly in Latin. See also Hale, *Precedents and Proceedings*, 23 (no. 123).

26. The scribe has written 1480, but this case is among the Commissary court papers for 1492–93. Perhaps the scribe left out an x in his date? In any case, the date remains unclear and could be sometime between 1480 and 1493.

27. *upon warantise*

mother and my children will be[28] undone." Then Richard Laukiston said "Deliver me the mazers and I will warrant thine intent shall be fulfilled." Then Margaret gave him 2 maplewood mazers[29] worth 5 marks and 10 shillings in coin. For which reasons Richard and Margaret appeared judicially[30] before us, Richard Blodiwell, doctor of law, and they were sworn, having touched the sacred gospels, to respond truthfully to the aforementioned articles and to whichever of them; they confessed all these things are true, just as these were written above. Then, after the Gospels were touched and both parties promised to perform the assigned penance, the judge imposed penance on Richard and Margaret. Namely, that Richard restore, or make restitution for the 2 wooden bowls or their value, to Margaret within 8 days under pain of major excommunication, which the judge assigned now for then and then for now.[31] The judge reserved for himself the remaining part of the penance until the morrow of the following St. Andrew's Day.[32] The judge imposed on Margaret a public penance, namely, that for three Sundays barefoot, with her head covered with a knotted kerchief, in a kirtle,[33] carrying a candle worth one pence in her right hand, she should proceed to the cross in procession.

3.4. LOVE POTION AND SUSPECTED BOOKS[34]

19 December [1527] in the register house [of the Bishop of London] Margaret Williamson is charged *ex officio* that she used a love potion and possesses suspect books. She appeared and confessed certain books of parchment were at the house of Henry Devell, and the official required her to produce the suspected books which she has at the next [session], she is dismissed.

---

28. *wer*

29. *murras*

30. I.e., in court

31. *nunc pro tunc et tunc pro nunc.* A legal phrase meaning the settlement is deemed retroactive and for the future.

32. November 30

33. = gown

34. LMA, DL/C/B/041/ MS09065J/002, fol. 45. Written in Latin. See also Hale, *Precedents and Proceedings*, 102 (no. 325).

3.5. THE CASE OF THE FANSOMES: LOVE MAGIC, ILLEGAL
MEDICAL PRACTICE, AND FORNICATION IN THE RECORDS
OF THE HIGH COMMISSION FOR 1589[35]

The personal responses of Thomas Fansome made to certain articles
given and administered through the High Commissioners of Her
Majesty the Queen against him and his pretended wife:
Having been examined, he answered to the first article that he was
married to his now wife named Alice Smith, the daughter of Clement
Smith of Castle Hedingham,[36] shoemaker in the city of Norwich in
St. Stephen's Church, she being before a maidservant in the house of
Daniel Hughes of Cockstall[37] in Essex, a wool comber,[38] about six years
ago and that he carried her to Norwich not above a week[39] before he
married her, and saith that he was asked three times in St. Stephen's
Church, as he saith, and was married the Monday, a week[40] after Easter,
[which] next coming shall be six years, by the minister there, whose
name was Robert Jonson, a tall man and big, with a brown beard, in
the forenoon between eight and nine of the clock in the body[41] of the
church and after went up into the chancel into a seat on the left side
of the chancel. And he saith that the minister said the whole service at
that time and did then wear a surplice, and that at his marriage, as he
saith, there was three or four who were with him to the church, whereof one was named Richard [167] Colt and one Buttfield, a bowyer[42]
dwelling at the Red Lion in St. Stephen's Street near the gate and two
or three of Buttfield's servants. Afterward he voluntarily confessed
that, in truth, he was never married unto the woman that goeth about
with him, whom he hath called his wife, but in truth he saith that he
hath kept company with her these six years.

---

35. Kent Archives and Local
History, DCb/PRC/44/3 fols. 166–169
and fols. 85–86. Very few cases survive
from the High Commissioners Court.
For general information about the High
Commission, see Roland Greene Usher,
*The Rise and Fall of the High Commis-
sion* (Oxford: Clarendon Press, 1913).
Text switches back and forth between
Latin and English throughout.

36. *Hemmingham*
37. Perhaps Coggeshall?
38. *woll comer*
39. *senight*
40. *senight*
41. = nave
42. = a bow-and-arrow maker, also
called a fletcher

To the second he saith he hath no dwelling place but sometime hath a chamber in one place for a fortnight and sometimes for a month.

To the third article he confesses it to be true saving that he was Doctor Burcott's[43] man, of whom he learned many things in physic which he hath put in practice. And he saith that he has a license from Mr. Doctor Aubrey by reason of a testimonial which he had under seal from Mr. Broanne the Mayor of Canterbury which he showed forth at this his examination. And [he] saith further that he had another testimonial before that from Sir Owen Hopton and another which Mr. Cobham did take from him. Afterward, he being urged and convicted by circumstances in his answers, he confessed that he was never Doctor Burcott's man but saith that he is a tailor by occupation.

To the fourth he confesses that he hath received money of divers [persons] for such things as he ministered unto them thereby hazarding the health of divers [persons] and abused divers of her majesty's subjects and did take of them money, apparel, and other things for his unlawful practices.

To the fifth, sixth, and seventh articles he confesses that at the request of William Suttyll's[44] wife he did give her a writing or a charm to make her husband to love her and that he gave another prayer to a cutler in writing which he did write with his own hand. And also, he saith that the prayer, conjuration, or writing which he gave unto Suttyll's[45] wife was and is his own handwriting. And further he saith that he gave Yetman's wife a like writing at her petition whereby she might procure my Lord of Dover's[46] goodwill toward [her] husband and saith that he had of her 6 s. 8 d. for the same writing. And [he] saith that he had of the cutler [168] five shillings and a knife for his writing and things which he gave him. And he saith further that he had of Suttyll's wife in money 6s. 8d. and his wife had two half kirtles and a wreathed ring of gemewes[47] of gold and a quarter of an old

43. John Bennell, "Kranich, Burchard [Known as Dr Burcot] (d. 1578), Physician and Mining Entrepreneur," in *Oxford Dictionary of National Biography* (Oxford: Oxford University Press, 2008), https://doi.org/10.1093/ref:odnb/52152.

44. *Suttyl his*
45. *Suttyl his*
46. *Dover his*
47. = a double ring

rial.[48] And he saith further that one Robert, one William White, and Thomas Young of Milton had each of them a writing or charm of him to get them love of maids or to procure maids to love them. Also, one Robert Forman of Milton was with him unto whom he told certain words which he should say and observe to get love of a maid which he meant to marry. But [he] did not marry with her, and as he saith, he willed him to go to her on a Friday at 8 of the clock in the morning and no other time, and of him he had 2s. Also, one William Thomson of Rye, a tailor, came to him and desired him to help his child because it was greatly vexed both day and night and could not sleep. And he saith that with herbs and oils he did help the said child and of the said Thomson he had 2s. And he saith further that Mistress Clerkson of Heath came to him in Heath to know whether she should have a young man or an old man to her husband and she told him, as he saith, that one Thomas Langdon kept her in her husband's days and that he, the said Thomas, was gone a warfare, and whether she should marry him or no. And he told her, that if she loved him, she should marry with him. And he sayth he [i.e., Fansome] lay in her house a night and had his supper given him but nothing else and the commissioners did not examine him further about the said articles.

The personal responses of Alice Fansome, alias Smythe, pretended wife of Thomas Fansome, having been made to the aforementioned articles given and administered against Thomas Fansome and her.
She answered and confessed to the first article that she was not the wife of the aforementioned Thomas Fansome and that she and the said Thomas Fansome had no certain dwelling place at any time, but have continued sometimes in one place a month, sometimes in another a fortnight. And she saith that the said Thomas Fansome, her pretended husband, hath given medicines or physic to diverse [persons] and hath dealt in diverse other matters which she knoweth not of as she saith and the commissioners did not examine her further concerning the given articles. [85]

48. *ryall* = a gold coin first issued by Edward IV in 1465 worth around 10 shillings; also called rose noble. After 1553 it was worth around 15 shillings. Gold coins were often cut, especially in quarters.

Acta before the Reverend father Bishop Dovor, Reverend Lord Archdeacon at Canterbury, and the Venerable Master Thomas Lawse,
Doctor of Law, Royal High Commissioners to ecclesiastical causes etc.
20th of March AD 1589 in the residence of the aforementioned Reverend Father, in the presence of me, Richard Walleys, notary public, etc.
On which day and place Thomas Fansome appeared in person
(attached by others and imprisoned in the prison called Westgate)
and the commissioners presented the written articles to him and by
oath they have charged the said Thomas Fansome, having touched
[the Holy Gospels], to faithfully respond to the same; and they have
advised him to undergo the examination upon the said articles
immediately etc.

The hour after noon of the same day Alice Fansome, alias Smythe,
pretended wife of the aforesaid Thomas Fansome, appeared in person
and the commissioners charged her by oath, having touched [the holy
gospels], to faithfully respond to the articles administered against
her and her pretended husband and they advised her to undergo
the examination upon the said articles immediately etc. Finally, the
commissioners having inspected and considered their prior respective
responses to the articles, and having administered and made others etc.
from the confessions by them and whichever of them, they decreed
as follows, namely:·

That[49] the said Alice Smith upon Saturday next shall sit in a court
wagon or cart and shall have a paper on her head wherein these words
following shall be written in great letters, namely: "For living in fornication many years with one Thomas a counterfeit physician." And
in that manner [she] shall be carried from Westgate to St. George's
Gate, and from thence back again to Westgate. And that from thence
she shall be carried or brought to Milton, alias Middleton, and there,
on Sunday, being the 29th of this instant[50] March shall stand openly in
the church in the forenoon in the time of divine service with the said
paper on her head from the beginning of morning prayer to the end
thereof in penitent manner. And from thence [she] shall be carried to

49. At this point the records shift largely to English with a few words of Latin here and there.

50. = the same March in which the case is being heard, not March of the following year

Gravesend and there shall be set over the water into Essex and never to return again into Kent. And that the said Thomas Fansome shall, on Saturday next, stand on the pillory at St. Andrew's Church door in Canterbury from twelve of the clock until three of the clock in the afternoon with a paper on his head having these words following written on it, namely: [86] "A long fornicator, a lewd[51] charmer, a counterfeit physician." And on Saturday then next following, which shall be the 28th day of this month of March, [he] shall likewise stand on the pillory in Faversham market in manner and form and so long [a] time as is aforesaid. And on the Saturday then next following, which shall be the 4th of April, he shall stand on the pillory in the open market at Milton, alias Middleton, in manner and form and so long [a] time as is aforesaid. And to certify of the due performance and doing hereof at the next session of the said commissioners or before etc. And the said Thomas [is] to be brought back again to the house of correction there to remain until he shall be enlarged or discharged etc. And further it is ordered that before their enlargement they shall pay all such reasonable fees and other duties whatsoever to the officers of this court as shall be by the said commissioners tied and assessed[52] etc.

And further the commissioners decree that the license he had shown to them be confiscated by them lest he, the said Thomas, should afterward go about as he had done, and under pretense of his license, should still practice the like knavery and deceive the people and do harm as he had done before, etc. And they did admonish him to leave his said lewd devices and practices, and not use them any more under pain of the law, etc.

51. = unlearned   52. *tayed and sessed*

THE MAGIC TEXTS

3.6. VARIOUS EXPERIMENTS FOR LOVE[53]

For love (F49 7452)
Take a hazel rod of one year's growth and say a Pater Noster, an Ave, and a Creed, Dominus deus noster,[54] and Dominus regnaull.[55] And then in the midst cut the rod and then say: "I conjure thee rod by our Father and the Son and the Holy Ghost and by the mother of our lord Jesus Christ that he or she that be smitten herewith shall yield to me love everlasting." Probatum.[56]

Alytere[57]
Take a nutmeg and fill it full of holes then sweat it under your left armhole three times. Then take some of your nature (81t592)[58] and some of your blood (b7462), being pricked out of the hill of Venus (52856)[59] at eight o'clock on Friday morning, and put that in the hole of your nutmeg and then let it dry under your arm. Then take and give her the same, grated in drink or meat. Probatum.

Alytere
Take the heart of a swallow and wrap it in a green silk cloth and carry it about thee. Probatum.

Another
Take the powder of an adder's skin and bear it in thy hand until it be warm with the heat of your hand. Then put some musk or some hot

53. London, British Library, Sloane 3850, fols. 148v–154v. For more on this manuscript and the cipher it employs, see the general introduction.
54. Lord our God. Possibly incipit for Baruch 3:6.
55. Probably a mistranscription of "Dominus regnavit," the incipit for Psalm 92 Vulg.
56. = *Proven*

57. = *another*. A misspelling of the Latin word *aliter*. The scribe spells this word in various ways below.
58. Context suggests this is semen.
59. In medieval palmistry *mons veneris* refers to the base of the thumb. The use of this term for female anatomy appears only in the seventeenth century.

smelling thing to it and what woman so ever smelleth it shall love thee. But thou must have some always with thee when thou art in her company. Probatum. [149r]

For love (F49 7452)
Write these words in a red apple, "colacus, dandie, meigdi," and give her it to eat. Et fiat.[60]

Alytere
Take the fat of a Eprawlduam[61] and [put] it in her own blood and dry it at the fire. And touch the party about the breast and she shall love thee above measure.

Alyter
Take a green frog and put out his tongue and put it under your [tongue] and kiss her whom thou lovest.

Alytere
Write these words in virgin parchment on Wednesday morning before the sun rise and touch her whom thou lovest. These be the words:

$$\cdot\, \mathcal{1} \cdot D \cdot \mathcal{U} \cdot \mathit{of} :$$

Alytres
Take a nutmeg and fill it full of holes and swallow it down and when it comes forth wash it clean and dry it and then sweat it under thy left armhole three times. Then dry it and grate it and give her it to drink. Et fiat.

To cause a woman to follow thee
Write the name of the woman in thy right hand with the blood of a bat. Et fiat. [149v]

---

60. = and let it be done
61. It is entirely unclear what this creature might be. Perhaps a mistranscription or copy from a faulty original.

To make a man or a woman to love thee
Take and write with the blood of a dove in parchment these names:
"tanill, favo, steri, nulchatria." And bind it about thy arm and whisper
in her or his ear.

For love (F49 7452)
Write these letters on Thursday morning before the sun riseth in thy
right hand or left hand: . D . is . no . et . ta . a . mabit .[62] M . d . a . ff . X .

Aliter (A7it29)
Write these letters in thy hand with the blood of a bat: . H . M . T . F .
R . O . And touch her bare breast (bi92 b93ste). Et te sequitur.[63]

Alitre (A7ite92)
Take three drops of blood (b74d2) of thy little finger (7it2772 f38g29)
and write your name on a piece of bread (b92ad2) and give it her to eat.

Aliter (A7it29)
Write in a plate of lead two fingers broad or more thy name and
her name whom thou desirest and therewith write or grave these
characters.

[150r]

For love (F49 7452)
Take the heart of a white dove and put it under a hen on Sunday
morning before the sun rise in an eggshell and take it up again the
next Friday morning at the same time and take thereof and give it to
whom thou lovest in earnest (7452st i8 2983ste).

Alitre (A73te92)
Write these words in an apple: "drdia, sculpa, donrita" or "bedia,
sculpa, dreata" or "ruel, stituel, elitict."[64]

---

62. *Et te amabit* is Latin for "and he/
she will love you." Possibly unwittingly
incorporated from a Latin original.

63. = *And she will follow you.*
64. Perhaps also a single set of
words including the word "or" twice.

Alitre (A73te92)
Take an apple and write these words: "selpa, telpade, preaind, drago" and give it her to eat and she shall love thee (hi9 t4 2it2 and sh2 shi772 7452 th2).

Pro amore (Pio8092)[65]
Take an apple and write these three names in it with the point of a knife: "Baganell, Lusifier, Sathanas." And these following and conjure the apple by these names which are written in the apple and what woman (w48in2) so ever do eat (2it) of it shall love (shi77 7452) thee. [150r]

For love (F49 7452)
Take virgin wax from the bees at the time the moon is not at the full by a week and more,[66] and keep the wax until the next Friday and that day make thee a candle in the hour of Venus and write about it with the blood of thy little finger these names of spirits. Then write the woman's name whom thou desirest. First write "allaphe," then the woman's name. Then next write "Barathies," and thereafter the woman's name. Then thrice[67] "Obeffies" and the woman's name. Then write "Ariex," then the woman's name. After all this, say this: "I conjure you gods which were sent in to the closed vessel that Solomon did seal. I adjure you by the womb of the virgin and by all things which are under heaven or that be in heaven contained that you make her obey me." Which conjuration being said, light the candle quickly and put it out again and bear it to the church and secretly put it under a stone in the church so that it cannot be seen and then let remain until the priest be gone home. Then come back again and take the candle up and put it under your armhole till some of your sweat and heat be thereon. And then say in this manner: "Even as this candle is made hot by my heat so likewise let her be made by my love." Then if she be near, she will send a messenger. [151r]

But keep thee away and speak not with her, nor do not hear her talk, but make thyself strange. But when the messenger is gone, hold

<hr/>

65. = for love. This seems likely to have been the intent.

66. That is, during a waxing moon, the conventional time to conjure spirits.

67. .3.ly

the candle in thy hand unlighted and read thy aforesaid conjuration. And if she come not, light thy candle quickly and put it out again and do so often and chiefly about the twilight with a repetition of the same conjuration and the whole world cannot hold her but she will come to thee. But take her and beware lest the candle burn out the spirits written about it for so it may come to pass that she may burn so hot in love that she shall die suddenly because she being so far off and could not come as you would have her. Therefore take heed and beware that none of the gods' names do burn in the candle. All this experiment may be proved at all times saving in the decreasing of the moon, but in the waning[68] may best be done. Probatim.

For love (f49 7452)
Write in thy left hand before sun rising and whomsoever thou toucheth will follow thee. These be the letters: ". n . L . V . B . f . F . V . H ." Probatim. [151v]

For love (f49 7452)
Write in thy left hand before sunrise these letters: ". H . L . V . B .F . I . C . I ." And touch whom thou wilt and she shall follow thee.

Aliter (A7it29)
Take a swallow and hang her up in the chimney when you have pulled off all the feathers and [it] being dry, guts and all, and make a powder and put it in drink.

Aliter (A7it29)
Take a cock sparrow and get out his tongue and put it in virgin wax and frankincense, and hold it in thy hand when thou sweat, and put it in thy mouth and kiss her (h39) and she (sh2) will love (74v2). Probatum.

Alitre (A7it92)
Take an apple that never touched the ground and write in it these names "anaell, catell, et saell" and after say this conjuration (cony59at3on)

68. The scribe seemingly confuses waxing and waning. Typically, conjurations must be performed on a waxing moon.

following: "Comerote pomum per omnes demons qui temptarerunt in paridiso vt quecumqs mvlyer te gustabet in amore meo accendeat. Donec octuntatem meam."[69] Probatum. [152r]

Another (1n4the9)
Take an apple that never touched the ground and make the same [apple] hollow within. Then take virgin parchment and write therein with the blood of the little finger (72t272 f3ng29) these characters, which must be done in the house of Venus. Say thus: "The daughter of such a man[70] burn in as hot love of me as the love of Jesus Christ did burn in the heart of Virgin Mary." Then put in the parchment wherein the characters be with thy name and her name written in the hollows of the apple and bury it in the dunghill and as it wasteth away, so shall her love burn and increase to thy desire. These be the characters.

For love (F49 7452)
I am your flesh and I am yours, as occasion shall serve, to use. Wherefore your flesh I never will, while life last, abuse.[71]

[To remove a tooth]
Take the oldest and greatest water toads that you can get. Kill [one] and take out the guts out of him & wash him clean and boil[72] him and skim them clean and take off them that doth swim above and put it in to a glass and dip in the top of your finger and so touch the tooth and he will fall out presently.

69. = *I conjure you apple by all demons that were condemned in paradise that whatever woman should eat you will burn in love for me so long as it is my desire.* Due to numerous errors, the sense of the Latin is only barely recognizable.

70. The intent is that the name of her father should be said.

71. This short rhyming couplet is evidently meant to be written.

72. *seath*

Another (an4th29)

Take the great toads that be black. Then take the guts out of them and wash them and put them into to an earthen pot and set it into the oven and it will dry to a powder. Then stamp it into a fine powder and so carry it about you and it will drive away evil spirits. And whatever woman or maid doth smell it shall be inflamed with fiery darts of Venus's love.

[Notes on magic practice]

Note that all experiments of love must be done in the increase of the moon and in the hour and day of Venus or Jupiter and especially when the moon is in Virgo, which you may know by a common calendar.

To make one to dance upon Friday and for all kind of play at dice or play at cards in the day of Mercury or Jupiter. That is, Wednesday or Thursday. And not this for a general rule, that all experiments must be done [with] the moon increasing.

How you must work with any kind of blood (b7462)

Take a empty-stomached[73] bat and exorcise her after this manner: "Camat, laiuac, amac, tacac, marback obiack, iamachaz, volmrith. I adjure thee bat by the Father, Son, and Holy Ghost and by all the [153r] comintations[74] of the world and by all the words that were spoken by the maker of the world that thou serveth me and be my help." Then say, "O thou angel, Adonay Heliot and thou angel Adonell, be you my aid-help that through you I may accomplish my desire." Afterward take a needle and prick then under the right wing and the blood in a vessel and say, "O almighty Adonay, Araton, Asuul, Helve, Helion, Effercen: Sadon, deus derius in finitus."[75] Jesus Christus be my help that this blood may have power, and profit me in this thing that I would bring to pass through the aid and help and assistance of the Holy Ghost to whom be all praise and honor and glory both now and for ever more. Amen. Amen. So be it. Amen.

73. *lere*

74. Intent unclear. Possibly *comminations* meaning divine threatenings, or *conjurations*.

75. Possibly a mistranscription of *dominus deus infinitus* = *Infinite Lord God*.

To try a virgin wh[eth]er she be with child or not (v29g38 wh29 sh2 b2 with ch3762 49 81t2)

Take the seed of a red dock[76] when it is dry and bid the same maid blow the fire with her mouth and in the meantime, unknown to her, cast the seed on that fire and if she be no virgin she will presently piss.[77] Et fiat. Probatum. [153v]

To know whether a womb be corrupted or no (w48b2 b2 c494pt26 49 84)

Take the fruit of lettuce and hold them unto her nose (h392 n42s) and if she (sh22) be corrupted she will piss (c494pt262 sh2 will p3sh2).

Aliter (a73t29)

Take the powder of chamomile and give it her to drink (h392 t4 d93nk) it: predictus efferctus soquetus.[78]

To know if a maid be a virgin or no (T4 k84we 3f 1 81362 b2 1 529g382 49 84)

Take vervain gathered in the house of Venus or Jupiter and put [it] under her and if she (sh2) be defiled she (def3726 sh2) shall not sit a Pater Noster while (s3t2 1 p1t9 84st92 wh3ll)[79] but will remove (928452). Et fiate.

To know a maid (k842.1.m1362)

Take a black[80] stone with the roots of red nettles and make powder thereof and give it her to drink and [if] she be a maid she pisseth (81362 sh2 p3s2th) or otherwise not so.

---

76. *redge docke* (*Rumex sanguineus*)
77. *Pish.* Possibly meaning to express contempt, but experiment below ("To know if a maid") has "piss."

78. Corrupted Latin probably meaning "the aforesaid effect following."
79. I.e., the length of time it takes to say the Lord's Prayer.
80. *iette*

To make a woman conceive (w48182 c48c252) and be with child
(ch3762)

Take the stones[81] of a boar and dry then in a close-covered pot so
that no air come to it. Put it in some warm place. Give thereof to the
woman at her going to bed with her husband and by God's help they
shall have a son. Et fiat. [154r]

Another

And if she would have a maiden child, she must take the matrix[82] of a
hare and the chap of a hare lying welded[83] as afore said. Et fiat.

---

81. = testicles   83. *lyng lynge welldide*
82. = uterus

CHAPTER 4

Men's Games

Gambling, Hunting, and Fishing

Hunting and fishing were understood in the premodern period as manly pastimes. They combine skill, raw luck, risk (since they were often carried out illegally), and the potential for bragging rights in a potent combination.[1] It is no surprise that men tried to enhance their luck with magic. It is also no surprise that where they occur in manuscript, hunting and fishing magic can be found collected together with their much more common cousin, gambling magic, which relies on a similarly attractive mixture of risk, skill, and potentially high dividends.[2] Gambling was also a largely masculine activity. Records suggest that, although women may have been present, the clients of gambling establishments were uniformly male.[3]

The collection "Of Love, of Kardes, Dies and Tables, and Other Consaytes" from which Text 3.6 is drawn clearly foregrounds gambling and love (by which it mostly means pursuing women for sex) as comparable and associated pastimes in which fortunes may be increased through magic. The collection also includes hunting and fishing magic. One hardly need point out the conceptual commonalities between hunting and men's pursuit of women for sex, and in the case of this collection such comparisons would be justified. The commonalities between gambling and hunting are also very clear. In fact, the first

1. Barbara Hanawalt, "Men's Games, King's Deer: Poaching in Medieval England," *Journal of Medieval and Renaissance Studies* 12, no. 2 (1988): 175–93.

2. For examples of Elizabethan entertainments such a card games, see Jeffrey L. Singman, *Daily Life in Elizabethan England*, Greenwood Press

"Daily Life Through History" Series (Westport, CT: Greenwood Press, 1995), 159–90.

3. Karen Jones, *Gender and Petty Crime in Late Medieval England: The Local Courts in Kent, 1460–1560* (Woodbridge, UK: Boydell, 2006), 58–59 and 189.

charm we provide from this collection (Text 4.3) combines gambling and shooting.

Gambling was an elite pastime and technically illegal for most people, but efforts to control it were largely ineffectual, something that made it similar to magic. In 1541, the Act for Debarring Unlawful Games made a feeble attempt to limit its practice, but exclusions and exceptions for the propertied class made the act toothless. In 1576, a new act consolidated control of gambling under the crown, and authorities returned to the older habit of licensing gambling houses and the importation of cards and dice.[4] At the same time, religious writers inveighed against gambling, and popular works describing the defrauding of foolish and inexperienced young men in London became a genre unto themselves. If this kind of moralizing proscription was not enough to enhance the attractiveness of gambling by making it a forbidden pleasure, the fact that prostitution was inextricably interwoven with the social world of gambling certainly did.[5]

The underworld of gambling and prostitution is manifest in the legal records containing instances of gambling magic and also in materials we have already examined.[6] The young Edward Underhill (Text 1.1) had squandered much of his patrimony in gambling. Although Underhill undoubtedly exaggerated due to his religious beliefs, the picture he paints of the underworld of gambling and prostitution is credible. So too are his claims about how magic and gambling were interwoven. By his account, the cunning man Robert Allen provided gamblers with magic to enhance their luck. Allen lived in the debauched house of a "great dicer" called Gastone, paying for his room and board with his magic services. In fact, Text 1.4, written on a scrap of paper Underhill confiscated from Allen, is a short work of gambling magic. The parallels with the story of Harry Neville (1525–1563) and his magician Gregory Wisdom, to which we now turn, are striking.

4. John L. McMullan, *The Canting Crew: London's Criminal Underworld, 1550–1700* (New Brunswick: Rutgers University Press, 1984), 40–43. For the act itself, see 33 Hen. VIII, c. 9.

5. Alec Ryrie, *The Sorcerer's Tale: Faith and Fraud in Tudor England*

(Oxford: Oxford University Press, 2008), 64–108.

6. For another example, see the case of Drs. Elkes and Spacie. NA SP/12/186/188r and 221–25. Cited in Macfarlane, *Witchcraft in Tudor and Stuart England*, 303.

Harry Neville's confession (Text 4.1) reveals him to be a typical instance of the spoiled and bored rich kid. He was young, idle, unhappy in marriage, and the heir apparent of the Earl of Westmoreland. According to his own confession, he led a dissipated life of gambling and whoring, or, as he put it, of "play and dally-doo." Due to his strong prospects, Neville also had easy access to loans and, like many in his position including Underhill, amassed considerable debts. He was first seduced into the world of magic with the promise that the magician Gregory Wisdom could make him a ring to bring him success at the tables. After several months of living in Neville's house, Wisdom finally produced the ring.[7]

Initial success in gambling convinced Neville of Wisdom's abilities, but he quickly began to lose money again. He claims in his letter of confession to have had growing concerns about his lack of success, but he still went on to pay for a magic operation to make him a great musician and gave Wisdom funds for a treasure-hunting expedition to his father's lands in the north. Despite Neville's vociferous claims to the contrary, he seems to have supported Wisdom's project of killing his wife and father by magic. We know this from a subsequent letter where he admits to this but claims to have been convinced by Wisdom that death by magical means was not so bad because his wife would certainly go to heaven. Predictably, none of this magic worked.

Wisdom was a better con artist than a magician, and by the time he had finished with the young nobleman, Neville had lost a considerable sum of money and was in jail, probably for debt, and was additionally suspected of plotting to use magic to bring about the death of his wife and father, a peer of the realm. This was treason plain and simple. But like most of those who found themselves in trouble with the authorities for practicing magic in this period (even treasonous magic), he was eventually released and, although chastened, was still ultimately able to take up his father's title.[8] Remarkably, Wisdom also evaded prosecution and went on to refashion himself as a physician.

7. For a full discussion of Neville and Wisdom, see Ryrie, *Sorcerer's Tale,* 20.

8. For the case of William Neville and on treasonous magic in general, see Klaassen and Wright, *Magic of Rogues,* 10–11 and 21–56. On treason and magic, see Young, *Magic as a Political Crime.*

His skill as a con artist no doubt served him well in this profession, and he ultimately managed to get a license from the College of Medicine.

Wisdom may not have been a "real" magician, but he clearly knew how to present himself as one. He was obviously familiar with the traditions of magic and used them to create believable rituals. Magic for gambling in various forms appears relatively frequently in magic books. The idea that rings had to be prepared at precisely the right astrological time so as to infuse them with the necessary powers from the heavens was also common. Wisdom also improvised with existing traditions of magic. The magic table he built for the invocation of Orpheus is clearly based on ritual magic traditions. His preparation of Neville's chamber follows the ritual magic tradition of preparing special rooms for conjuring.[9] His claim that Orpheus would appear as a small child follows the common practice in demon conjuring of commanding spirits to appear in nonthreatening forms. Finally, the hanging fabrics and "board of green wax with four tapers burning on it" are clearly based upon the Holy Almandal, an angel scrying device made of wax and supported by four candles that was to be employed in a similarly prepared room.[10] So Wisdom was undoubtedly familiar with magic traditions, even if he only used the magic books as source-books for convincing fraud.

By comparison with the rest of the material in this chapter, legal records of hunting and fishing magic are very rare and largely circumstantial. Edwin Hadslye, one of several men presented for poaching and assault in 1606, was accused of having offered Lord Morley information gained through his scrying glass about other poachers. But there is no evidence in this case, nor in two other cases of magicians who were also hunters, how magic was employed for hunting.[11] There are, however, two more compelling records.

9. See the "four-windowed room" of the *Thesaurus spirituum*: London, British Library, Sloane 3853, fol. 12, and Oxford, Bodleian Library, eMus 238, fol. 7v; London, Wellcome Library, Wellcome 110, fol. 62v. For magicians using this room, see Klaassen and Wright, *Magic of Rogues*, 87 and 117–18.

10. Jan R. Veenstra, "The Holy Almandal," in *The Metamorphosis of Magic*, ed. Jan N. Bremmer and Jan R. Veenstra (Leuven: Peeters, 2006), 189–229.

11. STAC 8-58-5. Cited in Macfarlane, *Witchcraft in Tudor and Stuart England*, 301. See Klaassen and Wright, *Magic of Rogues*, 40 and 103.

Text 4.3 concerns John Nooke, a cleric who "had a book about fishing, about walking about invisible in the nighttime, and about seeing at night just as in the day." The book clearly involves magic for night vision and invisibility, but it is not entirely clear whether the section on fishing was *fishing magic* or a text on angling. Nonetheless, it is worth noting that invisibility and fishing magic do appear together in the manuscript from which Texts 4.4–4.6 were drawn.[12] Nooke's book seems likely to have followed the same pattern. However, the only clear presentment for hunting or fishing magic alone is Text 4.2, in which two fishermen were charged with charming their nets. This was evidently regarded as a minor offense which the Dean of Wisebech's court sought to correct. The accused men managed to find oath-helpers who attested to their good character, and the cases were dismissed.

The relative rarity of these cases may be a function of the private nature of hunting or fishing magic and the fact that the only "victim" would be an animal. Charming an animal might have been a sin, and worthy of correction, but would not bring about the sorts of social disruptions attending something like divining the identity of a thief. Similarly, it was decidedly not gambling magic that got Henry Neville, Gregory Wisdom, and Robert Allen in trouble with the law but concerns about treason.

LEGAL TEXTS

4.1. LETTER OF CONFESSION OF HARRY NEVILLE[13]

To the Right Honorable and my singular good friend, Sir William Paget, Knight, Chief Secretary to the King's Majesty, deliver this.
After my most humble commendations and hearty thanks unto your Mastership for your great goodness showed to me at all times, humbly desiring you to continue the same.

---

12. Klaassen and Bens, "Achieving Invisibility."

13. NA SP 226, fols. 119–22.

This shall be now (as near as I can call to my remembrance) to declare unto you the whole circumstance of my grievous offenses. First, if it may like you to understand, Menville came to me a month before Christmas next shall be two years[14] and said these words unto me in my garden.

"My lord, I know that you are far in debt and know not which way to pay the same. Also, you have lost much money on play and dally-doo. But yet if you will follow my counsel, I can devise such a way for you whereby you may both recover your loss and also win as much as shall pay your debts and have enough to serve yourself besides from time to time."

And I asked him which way he could bring the same to pass. He said there were men that could by art make a ring that whosoever had the same upon his finger should win all that he played for, and he thought Stafford (if I would speak him fair) could help me to such a man.

Upon this, I sent for Stafford [to come] into my garden, who was at the same time ready to ride into the country to my father's, and thus I said unto him, Menville being by: "Stafford, as I have taken you always to be my assured friend, so now I desire you that you will show yourself the same. For Menville here declareth unto me that it is possible to have a ring made by such art that whosoever weareth the same shall win as much as he playeth for at the dice. Also, he thinketh that you can help me to a man that is cunning in that craft."

And he answered me, "My lord, I think I know where [there] is such a man. However,[15] there is an act against the practice of such things. Therefore, he will be loath to meddle with all and it is also dangerous for you to be of counsel in any such matter."

"What danger can it be," said Menville, "to any man as long as it is not known? And if it may be brought to pass, we shall be all made by the same, and able to recompense the worker."

Thus by Menville's crafty persuasions, and mine earnest desire, Stafford promised me [119v] to bring such a man in the morning to my house, and the next morning as I lay in my bed, Menville came to me in great haste saying, "My Lord, I can tell you good news, but you must

14. = almost two years ago   15. *howbehit*

rise straight [away] for Stafford hath brought the man he promised you, which seemeth to be both wise and wealthy, not in a threadbare coat as commonly these imperfect multipliers be, but well appareled like a cunning man in his craft. Therefore, rise and make you ready, for such rich men love not to give long attendance."

And this man which he brought unto me was Wisdom, whom I sent for in to my chamber as soon as I was up, saying to him, "I understand that you are well skilled[16] in astronomy and that by such cunning as you know you can make a ring that whoso[ever] weareth the same shall win all that he playeth for at the dice."

He answered me, "Such a ring can I make, but it is not wrought by astronomy, and yet I can work it two ways: both by a good spirit and an evil. But I will work it for you by the holy angels because it shall be of the more virtue, so that you will well recompense my pains, for I go about no such things but at the request of my dear friends, for most of my practice[17] is in physick. I dare say such a ring would be worth two or three thousand pound to you this Christmas. Therefore, I doubt not but you will give me at the least twenty pounds per[18] year during my life for my pains."

Then said I, "That is too much. But I am contented to give ten pounds by the year to be paid after my father's decease if it take effect, and in the meantime to reward you according as I win."

Upon that he was contented and said he would come the next day in the morning, but he must have four marks to buy all such things as were necessary for him, the which I gave him. Then Stafford took his leave of me and went into the country so that I saw him not for[19] a long time after.

Within three days came Wisdom to me again and lay every night (for the most part) in my house from that time till Christmas, and every day he went abroad, so that he practiced not the ring [120r] but only betwixt three and four of the clock in the morning and five and six at night, for he said that the angels could not be spared from their divine service all the day long. Therefore, they must be taken before their matins and after their evensong. And thus, continued he till Christmas

16. *seene*

17. *my most practise*

18. *the*

19. *of*

day in the morning when[20] he came to me as I lay in my bed, with the ring in his one hand and a patent in the other, declaring unto me that he had finished his work according to his promise, whereby I could never lack. And [he] desired me that I would sign and seal his patent, which patent I over looked and found faults: that he had made it so that he, from that day, should have ten pounds by the year. And he said again that although it was so made, yet would he require nothing during my father's life, but would stand to my reward, and that he had made it so to the intent that if I died before my father, that he might then have the same. And upon this promise, I signed his patent, and he delivered me the ring.

Then went I to Miles's house to dinner, where I played at the dice with Miles, Sir Nicholas Poyntz,[21] and Thistlethwaite. And there (as the devil would to blind me the more) I won thirty pounds, and at three of the clock I returned to my house again, where Wisdom met me and demanded how I had sped, to whom I declared that I had won thirty pounds and gave him forty shillings to drink.

Then said he unto me, "Yet will I do you more pleasure than all this, for if you will give me four pounds to buy such things as I must occupy,[22] I will before[23] tomorrow night make you play as well on the lute and virginals as any man in England. And this can not be done but only upon Saint Steven's day," which was the next day after. Upon that I delivered him four pounds and he went in to the town to prepare all things necessary, and came again the next morning at six of the clock.

Then hanged he my chamber all with green say[24] and appareled himself and me in long robes of green taffeta. Also, he made a board of green wax with four tapers burning upon the same. Then kneeled we down before the table, one against the other, he reading upon a book and I with a supplication in my hand, ready to put up to the god Orpheus, which he promised should appear [120v] to me like a little boy, to whom I should desire to grant me that request. And as we

20. *that*

21. For Nicholas Poyntz, see Alasdair Hawkyard, "Poyntz, Sir Robert (b. late 1440s, d. 1520)," in *Oxford Dictionary of National Biography* (Oxford: Oxford University Press, 2015), https://doi.org/10.1093/ref:odnb/70796.

22. I.e., acquire

23. *will or*

24. A wool cloth similar to serge, commonly used for curtains.

were thus kneeling, Sir Ralph Bulmar come suddenly in to my house, and would needs have come into my chamber, so that I was forced to cast off my robe and go out to him. And when I had dispatched him away, I came in again, bidding him to go forth with our business. Then he told me that I had marred all, for the hour was passed, so that it could not be done before Saint Steven's day come again. Thus departed he from me.

The same day after dinner I went to Domingo's to play at the dice, where I lost all that I had and came home in a great rage and I sent Menville for Wisdom to come speak with me, to whom I said that he had louted me and made a fool of me, therefore, I would have both my money and patent again. And he desired me to pacify myself, for he was sure that if I had lost, it was through my own default[25] and that I had had to do with some woman and the ring [was] on my finger, whereby it had lost its virtue.[26] And I told him it was untrue and fell out foul with him. Then desired he me to be contented and he would help me to money enough. For Menville told him that he was informed by a blind man, which was a Jew born and a practicer of the same art, that there was a cross beside a town of my father's in the north where lay a great sum of money, which he would get me. And that night would he speak with a spirit which he had in a crystal stone, and bring me word in the morning how much it was.

The next morning he came to me and said that there was two thousand pounds all in Portuguese, so that if I would give him and Menville twenty nobles to bear their charge, they would bring the same unto to me. And so, I dispatched them and gave them the money upon New Year's Eve, and Wisdom said that upon Twelfth Night they would be there and that I should know the same by a great wind that he would make to come into my chamber at that present time, which he bade me I should not be afraid of.

As near as I can guess, within three weeks after, came Menville to me alone and said they had overthrown the cross but they found

25. *defaute* = failure to fulfill an obligation

26. *his virtue.* It was common to require abstinence for the production of magical tools or to conduct conjurations. Generally, however, magic rings and other such items were understood to be efficacious after their production under any conditions.

nothing there. Also, he told me that Wisdom would not come to[27] me for fear lest I would beat him and that Wisdom said that I was so vicious that he could work nothing for me. And he [121r] came not to[28] me in seven days after. And then I told him I would believe him no more, for I perceived that he had gone about but to deceive me of my money and I was determined that he should deceive me no more. So had I rest of them both until the first week of Lent (as I can remember), that Menville and Wisdom came both to me when I was in the tennis play at Westminster, saying they must speak with me apart.

Then said Wisdom, "My Lord, I know you love not your wife, whereby you lead an abominable life in whoredom which will be your destruction both of body and soul, but if your wife were dead, then might you choose one which you might find in your heart to love and by that means lead an honest and a godly life. And here I have a book wherewith I can dispatch her and [it will] not [be] known but that she died of God's hand. Thus, I think, shall be the best way for you, for she, good lady, is sure to go to heaven."

These were my words to him again. "I would not for all the good in the world consent unto such a deed for it is both a sin against nature and against the Holy Ghost, which shall never be forgiven." And with this they departed both from me, I thinking nothing less than that they would have gone about any such practice, nor I neither sent for nor heard from Wisdom until mid-Lent Sunday (as I remember the day) that I met him and Menville by chance at Moorgate, where Wisdom told me that he had practiced the death both of my father and my wife, which words did so astonish me that I knew[29] not what to do nor say.

The first words I said were these, "I may curse the time that ever I saw any of you both, for you have gone about that (although I know it lieth not in your power) whereby you have undone yourselves and shamed me forever, for it will be thought that it came by my procurement. And so I departed from them so amazed that I knew[30] not what to do.

And straightways I sent for Wisdom's father to come speak with me in Morefields, to whom I said, "That villain, thy son, hath gone

27. *at*
28. *at*
29. *wiest*
30. *wiest*

about to destroy my father and my wife [121v] whereby he hath utterly destroyed himself and done his utmost to undo me."

And he quickly answered again, "If he have so done, I may curse the time that ever I begat him, and as for me I have nothing to do with the matter." And so he went his ways, and this can Old Wisdom not deny if he be a true man.

Then went I home, so troubled that I knew[31] not what was best for me to do, and the next day came Menville to me in my garden, desiring me that I would be good unto him and I answered, "How can I be good to thee, which hast gone about to destroy both my father and my wife?"

Then said he, "I take God to record, I never went about to practice it, but the offense that I have made you is that I was of counsel with him, and did not tell you whereabout he went." And so, cloaked he his fault with many fair words, ever desiring me to be good unto him, and would never leave me till I promised him that I would be good unto him, so that he would help me to take Wisdom. And so said he would and went straight to Wisdom's house, making me believe that, by a trick[32] he would bring him to me.

When he came again he said that Wisdom was taken hand and foot with a sprite,[33] that he could not stir, so that [he] was forced to keep [to] his bed. Upon that, I determined on the next day to take him in his bed, and make him sure,[34] and that done, to open the matter to my Lord of Suffolk. And according to this purpose the next morning at six of the clock, as I was going to Wisdom's house, I met him coming [at] a great pace, and as soon as he saw me he began to halt and draw his leg after him as though he could not go. When I came to him I gave him a great blow, saying his halting should not save him, and so hauled him out of Moregate by force, where he would go no further, till I would have smitten him with my man's dagger, which man did hold me and said, "Will you cast yourself away in killing such a knave?"

And I answered him again, if he knew what he had gone about to do, he would never hinder[35] me. These words can my man testify, who[36] went from me long ago and is now a Hackney man.

31. *wist*	34. I.e., restrain him
32. *a trayne*	35. *let*
33. = spirit	36. *which*

After that I sent Wisdom home to my house by that man and took Menville [122r] with me, going to speak with my Lord of Suffolk, who[37] at that time lay at the Barbican, thinking to open the matter to him and there to present Menville and after to have sent for Wisdom. When I came to the Barbican, I met Mr. Nawnton in the court, whom I desired to help me to speak with my lord, his master, and he said I could not speak with him. Then I told him I would give all that I had to speak with him, and he said again, if I would give never so much,[38] I could not speak with him, for he had been very sick all the night before and was then newly fallen asleep. All this I doubt not but Mr. Nawnton doth remember.

After that I went to my house again, where I found Wisdom locked in a chamber, to whom I said, "Thou mayst thank God that I can not speak with my Lord of Suffolk, but all shall not help thee for I cannot be at peace[39] till thou be hanged.

With these words he desired me to be good unto him and take pity on him for it should[40] do me small pleasure to cast him away, and also, although I were not consenting unto these matters, yet had I been of counsel both to the making of the ring and also to the overthrowing of the cross whereby I was as far in the danger of the law as he in all that he had done. All these words did he hear that was then my man, who I doubt not but can witness the same.

Then Menville and he kneeled both upon their knees before me, and with their crafty persuasions, brought me in such a fear that I let them both go, charging Wisdom that he should never come in my sight, and [I] dispatched Menville in to the country within two days after. And since that time, I take God to record, I have had nothing to do with either[41] of them but have abhorred them and all their doings.

And I shall desire you to consider that it is not <po>ssible for me to remember every word and hour of times and sayings two years past, and especially of that which I have abhorred to remember ever since. But as God shall judge me, I have as truly declared the whole circumstance, as my memory can serve me, of all my grievous offenses

37. *which*
38. I.e., no matter how much.
39. *in quyet*
40. The text repeats "for hit shulde."
41. *nother*

as touching these matters, for the which and all other, I ask God, and the King's Majesty, forgiveness, submitting myself [122v] unto his mercy and trusting to your goodness that you will be an earnest suitor for me and I doubt not, through the help and grace of God, but that from henceforth my life shall be such both to God and to the World, and with such a will to serve the King's Majesty that his highness and all others shall well perceive a willing heart in me to make amends for all offenses past if it may please His Majesty to show his wonted mercy upon me. And now I humbly take my leave of your mastership from the Fleet the xviiith day of November.

By your most bound Harry Neville.

4.2. ENCHANTING FISHING NETS IN WISBECH PARISH, CAMBRIDGESHIRE, 1463–1464[42]

Robert Mabley is charged with the crime of sortilege for enchanting fishing nets. He appeared on the 20th day of July and denied the article and has to purge himself six-handed[43] on Wednesday after the feast of St. Michael. On the day he appeared with John Gylot, John Hunt, John Warner, and William Pykard and others and he was dismissed.

   John Whitlamb likewise transgresses. He appeared at above and has to purge himself eight-handed on the said Wednesday. On the day he appeared with John Hunt, William Haldron, John Warner, William Pykard, John Austyn, John Herward, John Eylot and lawfully purged himself and was dismissed.

4.3. A RECORD OF A DEPOSITION BY WILLIAM FROM LEE INCLUDED WITH THE DORCHESTER ABBEY VISITATIONS IN THE DIOCESE OF LINCOLN 19TH OF SEPTEMBER 1530[44]

William from Lee says that John Nooke, a scholar at Canterbury, had a book about fishing, about walking about invisible in the nighttime, and about seeing at night just as in the day, which he sent with this

42. From the Deanery Courts of Wisbech. Poos, *Lower Ecclesiastical Jurisdiction*, 463. Written in Latin.

43. I.e., with six men to swear an oath to his innocence.

44. A. Hamilton Thompson, ed., *Visitations in the Dioceses of Lincoln, 1517–1531* (Hereford: Lincolnshire Record Society, 1944), 2:122. Written in Latin.

deponent [i.e., William], then staying at Denham, and this [deponent] loaned the same book to the parish clerk[45] of Hays in the archdeaconry of Middlesex, and when this [deponent] and also John Nooke again went to fetch the book from the parish clerk, the vicar of the village of Hays reproved[46] the same ones (i.e., William and John) for keeping the book and he said that they deserved <. . .> and then he gave back the book to John Nooke who <. . .> his relative[47] A. Purser in the town of Canterbury. And he said that Richard <. . .>mar saw the same book in the parish of Bray, and he offered 40d. to John Nooke for a copy of the book.

MAGIC TEXTS

4.4. EXPERIMENTS FOR GAMBLING[48]

An experiment for playing at cards, dice, or tables, or shooting
Write these words in virgin parchment with the blood of an owl, "Galiem Tantadrie (Gil32m Tigti6932)," and sew them into thy right sleeve and win at cards.

Alytre (Alyt92)
Write upon virgin parchment these words: "galiena, trabiebria." And put it in thy sleeve and if you do win, you shall win still [i.e., you will continue to win].

For dice and tables play
Take three leaves of mugwort and write these names thereon: "galla, cabafruit, lyn" and bind these leaves (72152s) about thy little finger. Et fiat.[49]

---

45. *holy water clerk*
46. [*repro*]*babat*
47. [*con*]*sanguineum*

48. London, British Library, Sloane 3850, fol.155r–155v. For more on this manuscript and the cipher it employs, see the general introduction.
49. = Let it be done

Another

Take the longest feather in a swallow's wing and, with the blood of a bat, write the names or words that follow: "dasarsen, Clabraviss, inpict." And no man shall win of thee.

Another

Take virgin parchment and write these names in it with the blood of a lapwinke[50] or a peacock: "galiei + curlebrie." Then sew them in thy sleeve. Et fiat. [151v]

To win at dice

Take the seed of fern and bind it about thine hand and wish and think what thou wilt and throw it [i.e., think the number you want and throw the die]. Probatum.[51]

Another to cast what you will
These be the names[52]

sator
arepo
tenet
opera
rotas

Write these words or names in parchment with the blood of a turtle dove and put them in a linen cloth and sew them in that sleeve that thou dost throw the dice with.

Another

Write these three words: "Damon, Coza, Teelara" in ivy leaves or ribwort leaves. And hold those three names written in three of the leaves within thy glove in thy left hand while thou playest, turning and winding the dice on the palm of thy left hand on thy glove three times

50. = plover
51. = Proven
52. This is a magic square and palindrome of unclear meaning dating back to antiquity and is perhaps the most common. It reads the same backward and forward as well as vertically and horizontally. Although it appears to be built from the letters of the first words in the Latin Lord's Prayer (i.e., *Pater noster*), it is also attested in the pre-Christian period.

with thy right hand, or then play saying, "Damani, Coza, Teelara, on pain of your damnation, I charge you in the name of the living God to make me win."

4.5. THREE EXPERIMENTS FOR FISHING AND HUNTING RABBITS[53]

To take fish
Take the root of daisies and frankincense and beat them small together and temper it with malmsey[54] and it will be like salve or honey and keep it in a box and therewith anoint thy bait on thy hook and the fish will come to it.

Another for the same purpose
Take the root of vervain and boil[55] [it] in wort[56] a good while and save them in linen cloth, the newer the better, and let it be nine- or tenfold or more that the water may not enter thereto. Then hold it in thy hand in the water and anon the fishes will come to it and then what thou wilt take of them. Probatum.

To take coneys[57]
Take the kidneys of a female coney in rutting time and dry them. Also take asafoetida and dry it well. Then take virgin wax and so make a ball with all these and put it in thy bosom. Also thou must have a fire box. And when thou comest where conies are in the burrows, strike a fire and light a wax candle, having it ready, and put the candle into the hole and the ball in thy other hand[58] and make it to smoke so that the smoke may draw down into the hole. Then take away the candle and hold still the ball and in thy left hand above and as they come out of the hole, take them with thy right hand for they will come to thy hand for truth.

---

53. London, British Library, Sloane 3850, fol. 161v.
54. A strong sweet wine.
55. *seethe*
56. The sweet liquid made from malted barley before fermentation.
57. = rabbit
58. The scribe repeats "and put the candle into the hole" seemingly in error.

4.6. AN EXPERIMENT FOR CATCHING BIRDS[59]

To take birds
Take barley and put it into very strong vinegar and then juice[60] of rue. And then cast it to the birds the barley where they haunt. Et fiat.

4.7. THREE EXPERIMENTS FOR GAMBLING[61]

When thou wilt play at tables or at dice, say as followeth:
"I conjure[62] thee Collubram and all thy fellows by him that made you sure, by this bond, by the living God and true God and by these names Agnus, Ovis, Splendidus, Remenson, and[63] Elay, and[64] Teco, Arhaton, Ririoth, that you come and make game without deceit and without any tarrying in that form or shape, which I shall command you, whensoever or wheresoever I shall command you at my pleasure by the virtue of these characters following."

"I conjure you spirits Lacandelicia, Bariacus, Bariake, Fordicat, Antheriache, I conjure and call you and I desire you as I hereof bear you, and I charge you, by the power of almighty God, and by the living God, three persons and one God in trinity, and I desire you by the virtue of these sanctified characters, that you make me to win of all creatures, so long as I have the names about me."

Bethelo: suspens in ethera, super ea empion, empe ge du pa melion, Anguis, nonis, Agrippis, fons, floressis,[65]

---

59. London, British Library, Sloane 3850, fol. 143v.

60. *Iyste*

61. London, British Library, Sloane 3846, fols. 33v–34r. The text is for the most part in English with some short Latin phrases.

62. Here and below his word is indicated by the Latin abbreviation for "con."

63. *et*

64. *et*

65. Most of this makes little sense. The first part of the phrase seems to intend "hanging in the ether, above it the empyrean." It is curious to see "Agrippis" as a word of power. It seems to be a reference to Henry Cornelius Agrippa, the best-known, most influential author on magic in the sixteenth century.

𝓂 ♏ ·♌·♄ ♓ ♋ ♄·7 ♄ orn desed baldechia, oo. ♈·☉ ♑ ♒ sapors, ara, lacandelicia, baracus, bariake, fordicat, Antheriache. boules & weprz Tbbqhhk dyse Cardes.

[Write] these names [fol. 34r] with the blood of a sparrow in virgin parchment or with the blood of a white cock[66] that has never copulated[67] or a pullet all white in her virginity. With the preceding experiment.[68]

Kill a bat and prick [her] on the right wing, but in [the] taking of her, let her not fall down nor touch the ground. Then write in virgin parchment these names following, and wear it on that arm thou playest withal.

o o + l + v + z + n + nol + am + pro + d + all + and[69] thou shalt win at all plays.

In virgin parchment, in the day and hour[70] of Mercury write "duncari, cora, telera, glassa, cela, essera, quill, bariell, Saggenell," and bind it to thy right arm and thou shalt win at all games, if you have some faith.[71]

Before thou take the blood, they must be enchanted alive, and so must virgin parchment be made in his hour and enchanted. When you play, set the moon on thy back, or else the lord of the artificial hour.

---

66. *Hic nomen cum sanguine passaris in pergamena virginea or cum sanguine galline albe*
67. *was never trode*
68. *cum prececente experimente*
69. *et*
70. *In pergamena virginea die et hora*
71. *si aliquam habes fidem*

CHAPTER 5

Healing and Protection from Harm

The female magic healer has been mythologized perhaps more than any other magic practitioner, and these gendered mythologies persist in modern scholarship. Cunning women have been employed rhetorically since antiquity as demonstrations of superstition and foolishness in opposition to which good (male) science, medicine, or religion can be constructed.[1] Modern studies have often tacitly followed this gendered view and have excluded or ignored considerable evidence for female practitioners of learned medicine.[2] Conversely, female herbalists and magic healers have been celebrated as the *central* providers of medical care in the premodern world. By some even less substantiated accounts these women were eventually excluded from practice by male clerical and medical establishments through the use of witch trials.[3] However, the realities are more interesting and complex. Recent scholarship makes clear that English women were just as likely to employ the medical techniques typical of conventional male physicians as they were to use charms or herbs.[4] As we shall see,

1. For a useful discussion of some aspects of these stereotypes, see Margaret Pelling, "Thoroughly Resented? Older Women and the Medical Role in Early Modern London," in *Women, Science and Medicine, 1500–1700: Mothers and Sisters of the Royal Society*, ed. Lynette Hunter and Sarah Hutton (Stroud, UK: Sutton, 1997), 63–88.

2. Doreen Evenden Nagy, *Popular Medicine in Seventeenth-Century England* (Bowling Green: Bowling Green State University Popular Press, 1988), 56–78; Margaret Pelling and Frances White, *Medical Conflicts in Early Modern London: Patronage, Physicians, and Irregular Practitioners, 1550–1640*, Oxford Studies in Social History (Oxford: Oxford University Press, 2003), 189–224.

3. For an overview of the divide between historical reality and modern mythologies, see Jo Pearson, "Writing Witchcraft: The Historians' History, the Practitioner's Past," in *Palgrave Advances in Witchcraft Historiography*, ed. Jonathan Barry and Owen Davies (New York: Palgrave Macmillan, 2007), 225–41. For a recent example of eliding witchcraft and healing, see Mary Chamberlain, *Old Wives' Tales: The History of Remedies, Charms and Spells* (Stroud, UK: Tempus, 2006).

4. Pelling, "Thoroughly Resented?," 82.

the sex of magic healers appears to have been evenly divided between women and men, and the legal evidence suggests that neither were subject to a great deal of interference from authorities.

Over the past few decades historians have increasingly incorporated magic into the history of medicine.[5] When sixteenth-century people were sick they might have sought out a variety of treatments from formally trained doctors (if they could afford them), barber surgeons, priests, empirics, or cunning folk, without any sense that their techniques were at odds with each other.[6] Although there is evidence people sought magic healers as a last resort,[7] practitioners across the spectrum, from cunning folk to physicians, employed magic techniques. Simon Forman and Richard Napier's practice included both conventional medicine and magic.[8] Late medieval university-trained doctors included collections of charms in their books.[9] And the placebo or expectation effect has been long known and discussed in medical circles and used to justify the use of magic along with more conventional treatments.[10] As we have seen in the cases of Thomas Fansome (Text 3.5) and Gregory Wisdom (Text 4.1), magical practitioners also practiced conventional physic, and Gregory Wisdom was not the only magic practitioner to clean himself up and acquire a license from the London College of Physicians.[11]

Common healers who employed magic were very rarely presented in ecclesiastical or secular courts, but combining these few cases with manuscripts gives us a fuller picture of their activities. The examples

5. See, for example, Roy Porter, *Quacks: Fakers and Charlatans in English Medicine* (Stroud, UK: Tempus, 2000).

6. Katharine Park, "Medicine and Magic: The Healing Arts," in *Gender and Society in Renaissance Italy*, ed. Judith C. Brown and Robert C. Davis (Georgetown, ON: Routledge, Chapman & Hall, 2016), 129–49.

7. Davies, *Cunning-Folk*, 104.

8. Ofer Hadass, *Medicine, Religion, and Magic in Early Stuart England: Richard Napier's Medical Practice*, Magic in History (University Park:

Penn State University Press, 2019); Kassell, *Medicine and Magic*.

9. Lea Olsan, "Charms and Prayers in Medieval Medical Theory and Practice," *Social History of Medicine* 16 (2003): 343–66.

10. Judith Wilcox and John M. Riddle, "Qusta Ibn Luqa's *Physical Ligatures* and the Recognition of the Placebo Effect," *Medieval Encounters* 1, no. 1 (1995): 1–50.

11. Kassell, *Medicine and Magic*. See also the case of Richard Jones, magician, alchemist, and physician. Klaassen and Wright, *Magic of Rogues*, 21–56.

presented below span over a century; to give a sense of how unusual they are, we can look to witchcraft presentments. Of the 1,203 cases of witchcraft and magic Alan Macfarlane cites in Essex documents 1560–1680, only 6 explicitly involve healing, and only 2 of those healers were women.[12] By contrast, charms for healing and protection are among the most common form of magic appearing in premodern manuscripts, where they are widely and richly attested. These charms closely resemble the descriptions of magic healers' activities found in legal records, where healers employed simple religious formulae and prayers. The "Three Biters Charm" described in the case of Agnes and John Panter (Text 5.4) also appears in a number of early modern English manuscripts, including the one below (Text 5.9). All this confirms that the charms appearing in manuscripts represent a common, widely dispersed, and extensively used tradition.

Another aspect of the common tradition was magic for the healing and care of animals. This is visible in this collection in Text 5.4, in which women attempt to employ magic to encourage an animal to enter a barn and to heal a colt. Healing animals through charms also occurs in Tudor charm collections such as the Antiphoner notebook.[13] These follow the same basic patterns as regular charms.

Together these legal cases and manuscripts demonstrate that a continuous tradition of charms originated in the Middle Ages and persisted through the sixteenth century with very little alteration in content. Charms employed short verbal formulae, usually religious and often from the liturgy; they also employed gestures such as the sign of the cross, short religious stories (*historiola*), divine names, and sometimes inscribed words or figures. They were commonly metrical or had patterns of repetition. All of these attributes may be seen in the examples below (Texts 5.7–10). Charms also blend together with the genre of textual amulets, which were often simply inscribed charms (Text 5.10).[14] On the surface, charms can appear silly or simplistic.

---

12. Macfarlane, *Witchcraft in Tudor and Stuart England*, 255–303.

13. Klaassen, *Making Magic*, 59–62.

14. Mary Agnes Edsall, "*Arma Christi* Rolls or Textual Amulets? The Narrow Roll Format Manuscripts of 'O Vernicle,'" *Magic, Ritual, and Witchcraft* 9, no. 2 (2014): 178–209; Don C. Skemer, *Binding Words: Textual Amulets in the Middle Ages* (University Park: Penn State University Press, 2006).

Closer analysis often reveals that they have been carefully contrived to evoke religious feelings and associations through a highly condensed use of religious language, stories, allusions, or symbols.[15] Prior to the Reformation, charms can be said to have functioned almost as a kind of unofficial lay liturgy because of the way they resonated with and reinforced conventional religion. After the Reformation, they commonly persisted in their old form, attesting to a lingering attachment to the old religion.

When the ecclesiastical authorities sanctioned people for employing charms prior to the Reformation, they were motivated by a desire to educate the faithful to use church-approved healing and to maintain the church's monopoly on spiritual power (Texts 5.2–4). After the Reformation, church court presentments continued to be about preserving a monopoly, but now it was God's monopoly. In the Protestant worldview, the power of supernatural cures lay entirely with God. Writers such as Reginald Scot use this point to emphasize that Catholicism was inherently superstitious, by attributing power to physical objects, people, and rituals rather than to God.[16] To put it another way, some shifted their concern with superstition to a concern with *Catholic* superstition. At the same time, instructions from the crown to the bishops and from the bishops to their parish clergy tended to separate Catholic practices and magic into two separate categories. Whether anti-Catholic sentiments may have motivated the *ex officio* presentments for magic we see in Texts 5.5 and 5.6 is thus unclear. But the fact that they were relatively rare makes it clear that church authorities did not regard controlling this sort of magic as a top priority. If they had, they could certainly have found a good deal more of it. Instead, in a pattern we have seen numerous times, they tended to focus on magic and other forms of misbehavior that were socially disruptive.

The Reformation did, however, have a direct impact on magic in one way. Magic practitioners often sought to remove Catholic elements, particularly Latin prayers or formulae and invocations of Mary or other saints.[17] The charms in Text 5.7 (except the first) seem

15. Duffy, *Stripping of the Altars*, 266–98; Olsan, "Three Good Brothers," 48–78.

16. Scot, *Discoverie.*

17. Klaassen, *Making Magic*, 12–14, 24–27, and 80–81.

to have been subject to this kind of editing since the medieval versions would certainly have included invocations of Mary in addition to the Latin prayers, the Pater Noster and Ave Maria, and the Credo or Apostles' Creed. By contrast, the ones reflecting the perseverance of the old religious formula may be seen in Texts 5.8 and 5.10, both of which derive from a manuscript written by a scribe with clear Catholic sympathies.[18] So people had access to a wide variety of charms and knew what to do to make the charms less problematic. The fact that all the presentments for healing magic in the latter half of the century seem to target people using explicitly Catholic charms suggests that eradicating Catholic practices was the primary concern for the courts rather than magic per se and that charms of a less Catholic variety might have been quietly tolerated.

Another form of regulation also began in the sixteenth century that may have had a limited impact on magic or at least on magic healers. In principle, all healers had to be licensed by one of three bodies: the bishops, the London College of Physicians, or the universities of Cambridge and Oxford. Royal acts required the bishops and the College to regulate the medical marketplace and exclude unlicensed practitioners. The presentment of Thomas Fansome as a false physician (Text 3.5) was no doubt motivated by this requirement. It is not clear from current research how many magic practitioners were affected by the efforts of the London College of Physicians, but it is clear that the efforts of these bodies to control irregular practitioners were largely ineffectual. The medical marketplace remained vibrant and multifaceted and offered multitudes of different treatments and cures.[19]

A second form of magic, protective magic, does not explicitly appear in the court sources at all, but it cannot be disentangled from healing magic.[20] The two were commonly collected together in manuscripts as in Text 5.7 but are also conceptually inseparable. The protective amulet fancifully attributed to Pope Leo (Text 5.10)

---

18. For more on this manuscript, see ibid., 18–27.

19. Pelling and White, *Medical Conflicts*, 136–88.

20. On later magic against witchcraft, see Brian Hoggard, "Witch Bottles: Their Contents, Contexts and Uses," in *Physical Evidence for Ritual Acts, Sorcery and Witchcraft in Christian Britain: A Feeling for Magic*, ed. Ronald Hutton (Basingstoke, UK: Palgrave Macmillan, 2016), 95–105. On sixteenth-century examples, see Frank Klaassen, "Three Magic Rituals to Spoil Witches," *Opuscula* 1 (2011): 1–10.

illustrates this by offering protection from misfortune, illness, false judgment, and physical or social attacks. In part, this power to fend off misfortune derived from the idea that charms could operate like an exorcism. The last charm in Text 5.7 seems to mimic the practice of rogations, in which the territory of a parish was ritually blessed by walking around its borders. The first charm in the same section invokes God to cast out and prevent any threats to the safety of the household. Its additional effect of paralyzing the thieves so they might be brought to punishment also hints at more aggressive forms of protection magic.

Charms for witchcraft, such as those we find in Text 5.11, seem to have grown more common in the sixteenth century, and this may be an indication of a shift in popular concern toward witchcraft as opposed to more traditional supernatural assailants: elves, fairies, and demons. They are similar to Text 2.9, which seeks to torment thieves into returning to the scene of the crime. These anti-witchcraft charms also illustrate how magic was understood as one of the elements one might use to protect against witchcraft, which Macfarlane counts among common "informal counter-actions."[21] Informal actions of this kind were also later formalized in the techniques used by the seventeenth-century witch finders.[22] These and the second operation in Text 5.11 remind us that protective magic and witchcraft were two qualitatively different things in the minds of sixteenth-century people. In fact, since the magic of charms was understood to draw on the power of God, and witchcraft on the power of the devil, they were opposites. Curiously, when people did attempt magical assault, it also may have employed reservoirs of holy power.

We include the case of Katherine Love, presented for employing the "dropping of the candles" (Text 5.3), as an example of a seemingly real effort at assault through magic. The love charms of the bawd Joan Beverly (Text 3.2) were certainly interpreted as negative by the men who claimed she had performed it. But she might well not have regarded it as assault and, more critically, may never have performed it in the first place. Similarly, we have only the claim of the lying and

21. Macfarlane, *Witchcraft in Tudor and Stuart England*, 103–33.

22. Malcolm Gaskill, *Witchfinders: A Seventeenth-Century English Tragedy* (Cambridge, MA: Harvard University Press, 2005).

conniving Gregory Wisdom that he actually performed magic to bring about the death of Harry Neville's wife and father.[23] By contrast, Katherine Love confesses to having made an imaginative and entrepreneurial use of drippings of consecrated wax, presumably from church candles. By putting these in people's feces she evidently believed she could cause them some kind of harm or discomfort. This practice is a curious variation on known elements in magic practice. Experiments using wax and also parchment commonly required them to be "virgin" (i.e., previously unused), and consecrated tools or ingredients are critical elements in much magic.[24] The use of feces in magic is also not unknown, and the technique was also employed by two women in Canterbury.[25] All the elements are thus associated with known practices of magic and have the ring of truth. Furthermore, unlike the Beverly case, the account itself offers no obvious reasons to suspect the accusation as false, although it remains possible that she decided it was better simply to confess to a set of false accusations than to make things worse by denying them.

One final feature of this case also makes it valuable as a point of comparison. Magic is commonly thought of as private, particularly in comparison to religion, and anthropologists such as Marcel Mauss have argued for this distinction. Katherine Love's magic certainly seems to have been entirely solitary, no doubt due to its malefic intents. By comparison, however, all the other legal cases in this book involve magic performed on behalf of others or with accomplices and by practitioners known in their communities. The owners of the magic manuscripts might well have operated in an entirely solitary fashion, although evidence suggests they also operated in active networks of exchange.[26] In short, if magic pursued individualistic goals, it was certainly not private in any strict sense, and it was quite public in others.

23. Ryrie, *Sorcerer's Tale*, 19.

24. The *Liber consecrationis* (*Book of Consecrations*) is a good example. For a sixteenth-century English redaction, see Klaassen, *Making Magic*, 102–8.

25. Jones and Zell, "'Divels Speciall Instruments,'" 55. For another example of a related technique from a ritual magic text, see Cambridge, University Library 3544, fol. 83.

26. Klaassen and Wright, *Magic of Rogues*, 16 and 143.

Like sixteenth-century magic manuscripts, most common magic was medieval in origin and firmly situated in Christian beliefs and practices. Readers seeking shreds of surviving pagan traditions in these pages will largely be disappointed, not least because by this time England had been Christian for over eight hundred years. However, John Panter (Text 5.4) seems to have communicated with spirits on the summer solstice, which suggests he was engaging in pre-Christian practices and that the spirits he interacted with were fairies. At the same time, fairies were commonly conjured at this time using explicitly Christian rituals,[27] and the choice of the summer solstice no more indicates pre-Christian sensibilities than the contemporary practice of Hallowe'en indicates knowledge of the meaning of All Saints' Day. More critically, Agnes Panter appears to have confessed her practices to the priest, which suggests a high level of engagement with Christianity. Finally, the most accomplished local cunning woman employed five Pater Nosters, five Ave Marias, and a Credo, making clear that their magic was very much engaged with Christian spirituality. Any pre-Christian content in these cases appears fragmentary, and there is no evidence of any coherent pre-Christian belief system in play.

THE LEGAL TEXTS

5.1. INCANTATION OF HORSES[28]

St. Mary le Bow [1527] William Brown is charged *ex officio* that he used the magic arts and incantation of horses. He appeared and confessed that he collected certain herbs and he purchased others and he said the Lord's Prayer five times, the Angelic Salutation five times, and three Symbols of the Apostles. And these medicines cured the horse from the disease called "the fashyns." The judge ordered him to the next session in order to hear his will.

27. Klaassen and Bens, "Achieving Invisibility."

28. LMA, DL/C/B/041/MS09065J/002 fol. 52. Written in Ltin. See also Hale, *Precedents and Proceedings*, 102.

5.2. CURING A VEXATION OF THE MIND, 1510[29]

Also, [John Steward] saith that Thomas Laton came once to him to Knaresborough to seek a remedy for a vexation that he had in his mind by night and by day. His kinsman Paul showed him that the said Laton had used invocations afore and brought him a book of Laton's that he calls a "speculative" but he delivered it [to] him again incontinently. He saith that the book was of astronomy. He saith that Laton was well eased by such things as he gave him in medicines of spices and herbs and words of God together, which was the gospel on the Ascension Day. He says that he believes steadfastly that these things, with other prayers and good deeds that he bid him do, did ease him. Also, he saith that when persons and people came to him to have knowledge of things lost and stolen, he would show them a book of astronomy and make them believe that he was cunning. He could do nothing,[30] but sometimes it happened, as he said, and that was as the blind man cast his staff,[31] and some would give him money, and some wax, wherewith he kept certain lights in the church.[32]

5.3. FECES AND CANDLE DROPPINGS FOR HARMFUL CHARMS, 1499[33]

In the name of God amen. Before you Master Thomas Gilbert, vicar general to my lord of Bath, I Katherine Love of the city of Wells, curse, damn, and abjure all manner of heresies or errors [of] witchcraft and all superstitious sects and in special that I have used any charms and droppings of holy candles in man's or woman's seges,[34] believing that so doing I should harm[35] the person or persons that made the siege. For the which I am sorry of now, and I promise[36] and swear by

29. York, BIA, Abp. Reg. 26, fol. 72r. For more on this case, see Klaassen and Wright, *Magic of Rogues*, 83–116.

30. *no thing do*

31. I.e., like the blind man who hit his target by accident.

32. It is not unreasonable to assume that he had difficulty making ends meet and tried to supplement his income (and even funds for the care of the church) in this way.

33. Taunton, SRO D/D/breg/9 Oliver King fol. 51. See also Henry

Maxwell-Lyte, ed., *The Registers of Oliver King, Bishop of Bath and Wells, 1496–1503, and Hadrian de Castello, Bishop of Bath and Wells, 1503–1518,* Somerset Record Society 54 ([Frome, UK]: Butler & Tanner, 1939), 4. In English and Latin.

34. MED, s.v. sẹ̄ge n. 2.c. Guy de Chauliac's ME treatise uses the term "sege" to mean a bowel movement.

35. *noie*

36. *promytte*

the Holy Trinity and by these holy Gospels that I shall believe[37] here after as the holy church teacheth, and never use charm or dropping of candle in any sege hereafter or any other heresy or witchcraft. In witness whereof I make a cross for my sign to this mine abjuration +

This public abjuration by Katherine Love was read and made in the palace of the reverend father at Wells, before the venerable master Thomas Gilbert, doctor of decrees, vicar general of the Reverend Father Sir Oliver, Bishop of Bath and Wells, on the 13th of September, 1499, in the presence of Master John Bukland, Sir William Drewe, priest, John Bartilmewe, literate, and Robert Wyllyamson, notary public, and the lord enjoined upon her a penance to go before the procession into the church of St. Cuthbert, Wells, on next Sunday the 15th of September, in a shift, with bare head and legs, carrying an unlit candle called a "mache" and another lighted candle. And she was instructed to leave the town by next Tuesday and not to stay within seven miles of the city, under pain of greater excommunication.

5.4. ACCUSATIONS OF ENCHANTMENT AND CONSULTING DEMONS, 1514[38]

Consistory of the oft-said reverend father held in the said chapel on the eighteenth day of the month of April in the year of the lord one thousand five hundred fourteen.

John Panter, Doulting,[39] Sortilege

It was discovered by the bishop's official that John Panter from the parish of Doulting was accustomed to go to Mendip on the Vigil of St. John the Baptist for the purpose of consulting demons and to have answers from them; and he was captured there by William Zely of Shepton Mallet and others from the same parish who were accustomed annually to capture and punish such consulters.

---

37. *shalbe live*
38. Taunton, SRO D/D/ca/1a fols. 60v–61r. For an early partial transcription, see Aelred Watkin, ed., *Dean Cosyn and Wells Cathedral Miscellanea*, Somerset Record Society 56 (Frome, UK: Somerset Record Society, 1941), 157. Written mainly in Latin and occasionally English.

39. A village and parish two kilometers east of Shepton Mallet in the Mendip district of Somerset.

Sir Vaghan [with respect to] Panter

On the same day the official directed Sir Richard Vaghan and directed John [Panter of] Doultyng to appear on next Monday, namely the tenth day of April, since Richard was defamed, it was said, for revealing a confession, so that he should purge himself with four members of his order;[40] and so that John Panter should answer about [matters] touching illicit wandering to Mendip, as above.

The purgation of Sir Richard Vaghan, Priest

On the tenth day of the month of April 1514 in the said chapel, Sir Richard Vaghan, curate of the church of Doulting in the dioceses of Bath and Wells, appeared in person before the lord [Official] and he swore, while touching the Bible, that he never revealed the confession of Agnes Panter. And Richard, thus defamed, produced the vicars Sir John Mynlove and Sir Jacob Dole and his compurgators, having sworn bound by the law that they believed Richard has sworn the truth, as they had stated.

The Examination of Agnes Panter

On the same day there appeared before the lord [Official] Agnes Panter from the aforementioned parish, [because she] was detected concerning sortilege; [she was] sworn to answer certain articles etc. Asked whether she had practiced sortilege or had any communication with other women surrounding sortilege and she said no, except that she had set down a girdle[41] at the door of the barn[42] so that a certain cow would love the barn and she said that after the girdle was set down the cow intemperately did not go back, nor did she believe that cow to have entered more quickly through the placement of the girdle. And [she said] that Joan Bryant said to her and her husband that Margery Sevier the wife of William Sevier of Doulting said these words: "I have

---

40. *quarta manu* = four men from his order who will take an oath that he is innocent

41. *zone* = a woman's belt, not as in modern times an undergarment. Belt or possibly waistcoat. For other examples of magical garments, see

Maeve Brigid Callan, *The Templars, the Witch, and the Wild Irish: Vengeance and Heresy in Medieval Ireland* (Ithaca: Cornell University Press, 2015), 95. See also Scot, *Discoverie*, book 3, chap. 9.

42. *domus*

charmed a colt but I forget to charm me self." And then, Margery, in the perverse manner of sortilegers, procured vomiting, as she [i.e., Agnes] heard from the report of Joan Bryant.

The Examination of Joan Bryant

Joan Bryant, alias Fostell, of Doulting aforementioned, sworn on the same day and in the aforementioned place, denies that the aforesaid girdle was put set down by her counsel. Asked about Margery Sevier, whether she [i.e., Margery] was an enchanter, she said Margery used the aforesaid words "I have charmed a colt," etc. but this witness [i.e., Joan], asked about the vomit, as above, denied it.

The Examination of Margery Sevier

Margery Sevier, on the same day and place of the parish named above, was sworn before the lord [Official]. She said that Agnes Panter set down the girdle, as she saw, and she said that Agnes did this intentionally so that the cow would love its barn. Asked about the colt of William Gowle, she said that she [i.e., Margery] was sought out to cure the said colt by John Gowle and she said that she replied that she could not cure the colt through "le charmes" like her father was able to do while he lived, but that a certain Christina was learned and knew how to state[43] three or four words to recover the health of the colt from the teachings of this witness's [Margery's] father and from the grandfather of the same Christine. This witness confessed that she attended to healing the colt through "le charmes" but she forgot to care for herself through "le charmes." She was asked about the method of caring for herself and she said that whoever wishes[44] a suffering animal to be restored to health, it behooves that one thus to say "from man's bite, woman's bite, and all manner of beast's bites. In the worship of the Father, Son, and Holy Ghost, five Pater Nosters, five Ave Marias, and a Creed."[45] And then when she had vomit, as she says, because she did not know how to cure herself according to [her] art, as whoever

---

43. *perferre*
44. *volens.* We have adjusted the tense here to amend the poor grammar of the scribe.

45. *from manys bytt womans bytt & al maner of bestis bytt In the worshyp of the father son & holy goste v. pater noster v. aue marias & a cred.*

using "le charmes" around curing animals will have, as this witness confesses, as she says.[46]

On the same day the lord [Official] absolved Agnes Panter, who had been convicted for setting down the girdle, bound by the law in the same parish to say five Pater Nosters, five Ave Marias, and one Creed on her knees on the next Wednesday, Friday, and Saturday.

5.5. HEALING WITH PRAYERS[47]

[Archdeaconry of Suffolk, Deanery of Orford] Court held Friday, 11 November 1597, in Snape Church, with Thomas Mitfielde present as apparitor.[48]

Aldeburgh. Margaret wife of Neale.[49] She taketh upon her to cure diseases by prayer, and therefore hath recourse of people to her far and nigh. [She confessed] that she useth a prayer to God and then the paternoster, the creed, and another devised prayer,[50] and before these she is in the habit of washing.[51] Ordered to do penance in Alborough Church having a paper on her breast written in capital letters "for witchcraft and enchantment" with a white rod in her hand.

5.6. PRAYERS FOR ALL SICKNESSES[52]

[Maidstone, Kent, 1557] Cowdale being of the age of a hundred years is suspected of enchantment and witchcraft and being examined saith that he healeth people only by prayer having no respect to the manner

46. We have preserved the poor style and ambiguities of the Latin in our translation. *Et tunc cum habuit vomitum ut dicit quia non scivit artificialiter curare seipsam ut quilibet occupans le charmes circa animalia curanda habebit ut ista iurata confitetur ut dicit.*

47. Williams, *Bishop Redman's Visitation*, 1597, 133–34; P. E. H. Hair, *Before the Bawdy Court: Selections from Church Court and Other Records Relating to the Correction of Moral Offences in England, Scotland, and New England, 1300–1800* (New York: Barnes and Noble Books, 1972), 133.

48. An ecclesiastical apparitor was like a sheriff or bailiff in the secular courts; in the earlier Roman Catholic courts the apparitor would be called the summoner.

49. Margaret's husband's first name is not recorded.

50. *an other prayer devised*

51. *useth to washe*

52. Kent Archives and Local History, DCb/J/Z/3/32 f 203v. See also W. Sharp and L. E. Whatmore, eds., *Archdeacon Harpsfield's Visitation, 1557* (London: Whitehead, 1950), 216.

of the sickness, appointing five Pater Nosters, five Aves, and a Creed to be said in the worship of God the Holy Ghost and Our Blessed Lady.

THE MAGIC TEXTS

5.7 HEALING AND PROTECTIVE CHARMS[53]

An approved night spell[54]

> Holy God in trinity
> As wishly[55] I believe in thee,
> With thy virtue and thy might,
> Save this place both day & night
> Both within & without
> In every place round about
> From all enemies & from thieves,
> and from all men that untrue is.
> God with the virtue of thy right arm,
> Save this place from harm.
> God as well as I have in thee believing
> Save me and all my things,
> And if here come any thief
> Or any man that is untrue,
> I conjure him by the trinity,
> One God in persons three:
> Father, Son, and Holy Ghost,
> That virtue is of all things most,
> That is beginning and ending,
> And by the virtue of every thing
> That was and is and ever shall be
> Ordained by the virtue of the Trinity,
> By Heaven, Earth, Hell, water, and land,

53. London, British Library, Sloane 3846, fols. 74r–75r.

54. Although written in prose form in the manuscript, this has been presented in poetic form to highlight the rhyme scheme, which is consistent except for lines 13–14.

55. = steadfastly

And by all that was wrought by God's hand,
By word, herb, and tree,
And all things that may be,
And by the virtue of every sacrament
That is of God's judgment,
And by the virtue of every Mass,
That ever was said more or less,
And by all the virtue that God hath wrought,
That ever was said that ever was thought
And if here come any[56]
soon that would me
rob, or slay
or will these days
of my goods or me
In any wickedness deceive,
Stand they shall as any stone,
And have no power hence to go,
God then send them no power
For to go far or near,
Neither to look neither to speak
Nor on any creature them to wreak,
Neither by night nor by day,
'Til I bid them go away.
God grant me
All these things, thus to be
As I believe truly in thee
And in the worship of the Trinity.

Then say a Pater Noster, an Ave, and a Creed. Probatum.[57] [74v]

For a burning or scalding say:

There came two angels forth of the West.
The one brought fire, the other brought frost.

---

56. The line breaks are conjectural
here and in the next nine lines as the
rhyme scheme is not strong.

57. = Proven

Take out the fire and put in the frost
In the name of the Father, the Son, and the Holy Ghost. Probatum.

To assuage the venom of any prick or thorn

Our Lord Jesus Christ of the virgin was borne.
The Jews pricked him with brier & thorn.
Yet did it never ache, swell, nor rebel.
(Then name the party pained & the member pricked)[58] never shall
by the might of Jesus Christ.

Say it three times and three Pater [Nosters]. Probatum.

For the worms
In the hour of Lord, benidicite,[59] our Lord met with Rabbi, St. Peter's
brother. "Where hast thou been?" "At the land of nine worms." "Turn
again. Rabbi, and slay those worms every one from nine to eight from
eight to seven from seven to six from six to five from five to four from
four to three from three to two from two to one from one to none.
Thus slay these worms every one.
Say this 9 times.

For a swelling

Sweet Jesus on the earth was found,
He was beaten he was bound,
He was pricked he was stung,
Yet he never swell nor bell[60]
By the grace of him no more this shall.

9 times.

For a stitch
Abraham lay and slept under Mount Olivet. Jesus came him by.
"Sleepest or wakest, Abraham?" "I sleep not, Lord, nor wake not. I am

---

58. Instructions to insert the name
of the person and the part affected. The
lines could thus read, "Yet did it never
ach, swell, nor rebell. / Frank's index

finger never shall / by the might of Jesus
Christ."
59. = bless you
60. = swell up like a boil

so pricked with a stake." "Rise up Abraham & follow me. There shall never stake dare thee nor no [for] man that can say these words. In God's name, Amen."

3 times. [75r]

For a bleeding

O lord Jesus Christ that was in Bethlehem born
And baptized in the water of ye flood Jordan,
The water was wild and wood,[61]
Through the virtue of this child, the water stood.
In the name of the Father, the Son, and the Holy Ghost, stint may
   this blood.[62]

Say this 9 times.

A charm for thieves

I betake the Holy Ghost this place for to set,
To the Father and the Son thieves for to let.[63]
If any thief or thieves come my goods for to fetch,
The Holy Ghost before him or them for to let,
And there for to stand until I come again
Through the virtue of his holy name:

τελοσ[64]
Aggla, Agglitta, Adonay Oponymas,
Toy, tarta, Grammatis, Goddebris,
in meis erant[65] in nomine
patris et filij et spiritus sancti.[66]
τελοσ

---

61. = violent
62. = may this blood cease flowing
63. = impede
64. = telos (i.e., the end toward which something naturally moves). This Greek word is not a typical divine name, and why it brackets these final lines is not clear. Perhaps God is the

telos for humans or punishment is the *telos* of the thief.
65. = they were in mine. The meaning is unclear. Possibly a shortened version of "they were in my [i.e., God's] eyes." Cf. Isaiah 49:16.
66. = in the name of the Father and of the Son and of the Holy Spirit.

Read this 3 times as the sun is setting, going once round the ground.

5.8. AN EXPERIMENT FOR WOUNDS[67]

Take a piece of lead and on it say this prayer. "Lord Jesus Christ that with thy precious blood hath ransomed us sinful men on the cross, send thy blessing on this lead, that whatsoever sicknesses or wounds it toucheth after this time, through the virtue of the holy passion that he may receive health. Amen. In nomine patris et filii et spiritus sancti. Amen."

Then say five Pater Nosters, five Aves, and one Creed, and make of the lead a four-cornered lead plate in this form, with five crosses. And at every cross say a Pater Noster in the worship of the five wounds of our Lord Jesus Christ. Amen.

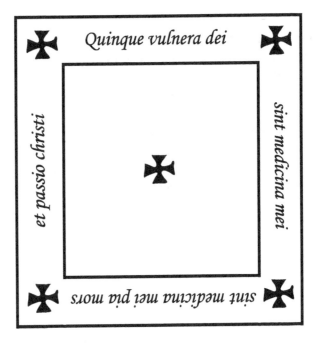

67. Oxford, Bodleian Library, Additional B. 1., fol. 20.

[Caption:] The Latin formula reads: + *Let the five wounds of God* + *be medicines to me.* + *As medicines to me, let the dutiful death* + *and passion of Christ be.*[68]

Then, setting the plate to the wound or to the sore, say thus: "As verily as the wounds of Jesus Christ rankled not, neither rotted, neither worms engendered, neither fester nor canker, nor no venomous matter,[69] so this wound or sore neither rankle nor rot nor fester, nor canker nor venomous matter may it grow,[70] but Christ Jesus through his might perfectly heal it. Amen."

And then say this prayer following. "Almighty God, everlasting health of all them that in[71] thee have believed, hear thou the prayer of thy servant whom we beseech thee to help of thy great mercy, that when he is whole he may give thee laud and praise in the holy church through Jesus Christ our savior and redeemer. Amen."

5.9. THE THREE BITERS CHARM[72]

[For one] bewitched or forespoken[73] or enchanted
If any three biters have thee forbidden,[74] with wicked tongue, with wicked thought, or with wicked eyes all the most, I pray God be thy boot.[75] In the name of the Father, and of the Son, and of the Holy Ghost, God that set virtue between water and land be thy help and succor with this prayer that I can,[76] for Jesus sake and St. Charity. Amen. Say this nine times over and at every third time a Pater Noster, and Ave, and a Creed.

68. This is a very common prayer. See, for example, the version from Sloane 3160 quoted in Tony Hunt, *Popular Medicine in Thirteenth-Century England: Introduction and Texts* (Cambridge: D. S. Brewer, 1990), 98.

69. I.e., it did not engender festering, a canker, or venomous matter.

70. *greene*
71. *on*
72. Oxford, Bodleian Library, e Mus. 173 fol. 63r.
73. = cursed
74. = cursed
75. = deliverance or remedy
76. = know

5.10. A PROTECTIVE AMULET[77]

Saint Leo, the pope of Rome, wrote these names to King Charles of France when he went to the battle of Roncesvalles and said:[78] the man that beareth these words upon him, that day he shall have no dread of his enemies to be overcome in battle, nor shall he never be burned with fire, nor drowned with water, nor he shall never die in strife and hatred, nor he shall never die sudden death, nor there shall never no wicked spirit hurt him, nor he shall never have sickness, neither the aches or the fevers, nor he shall never be falsely damned before any judge, nor he shall never have wrath of man or woman without great guilt, nor he shall never miscarry in no need, nor he shall never have disease[79] of thundering nor of lightning, nor fear his traveling, nor he shall never have the falling evil,[80] nor he shall not die though he were hanged (and that was proved by Tresilian, the justice of London). And if a woman be in traveling of child and she bear these names upon her, the woman shall be delivered, and the child shall come to Christendom and the woman to purification[81] through the virtue of these holy names of our Lord Jesus Christ following.

Original:
Iesus + Christus + messias + sother + Emanuel + Sabaoth + Adonay + vnitas + Trinitas + sapientia + via + vita + veritas + virtus + Opus + homo + Vsion + Saluator + Caritas + Æternitas + Creator + redemtor + Requies + finis + vnigenitus + fons + spes + sacerdos + ymas + Otheos + origo + manus + splendor + lux +

Explication:[82]
Jesus + Christ + Messiah + Savior (Greek) + God with us (Hebrew) + Lord of Hosts (Hebrew) + Lord (Hebrew) + Unity + Trinity + Wisdom + Way + Life + Truth + Power + Work + One Substance (homousion, Greek) + Savior + Charity + Eternity + Creator + Redeemer + Rest + End + Only Begotten + Font + Hope + Priest

77. Oxford, Bodleian Library, Additional B. 1, fol. 18r–18v. For more on this charm, see Klaassen, *Making Magic*, 49–50.
78. *say*
79. = fear
80. = epilepsy

81. I.e., the child will live to be baptized and the woman to be churched.
82. English equivalents or translations inserted where relevant. The source language is Latin unless otherwise noted. Some of the words are purely fanciful and so remain untranslated.

gracia + fons + mundus + imago
+ paracletus + columba + corona
+ Propheta + humilitas + fortis-
simus + altissimus + paciencia +
athanatos + kyros + yskyros +
et mediator + A + G + L + A +
Tetragramaton + caput + Alpha
+ et omega + primogenitus +
et nouissimus + panton Craton
+ et ysus + ego sum qui sum +
agnus + ouis + vitulus + serpens
+ Aries + leos + vermis + vnus
pater + vnus filius + vnus spirtius
sanctus + Ely + Ely + Ely + lamaz-
abathani + Iasper fert aurum +
Thus Melchior, Antropa mirram
+ hæc quicumque tum secum
fert nomina regum + Soluitur
a morbo domini pietate caduco
+ Ananizapta + Ananizapta +
Ananizapta + Iesus nazarenus
rex Iudeorum filij dei miserere
mei amen + Sana me et salua
me et costodi me domine deus
meus ab omni malo et ab omnibus infirmitatibus meis amen +
Michael + Gabriel + Raphael +
Saraphiel + Sariel + [19r] Vriel
+ Tobiel + Barathiel + Reguel +
Deus abrahami + Deus Isaacci +
Deus Iacobi + Petrus + Paulus +

+ Ymas + God (Greek) + Begin-
ning + Hand + Splendor + Light
+ Grace + Font + World + Image
+ Paraclete + Dove + Crown +
Prophet + Humility + Strength
+ Highest + Patience + Immortal
(Greek) + Lord (Greek) + Mighty
One (Greek) + and Mediator +
Thou Art Mighty Forever Lord
(Acronym of Hebrew phrase) +
Tetragrammaton (= the name for
the four-letter Hebrew name for
God) + Head + First (First letter
of Greek alphabet) + and Last
(Last letter of Greek alphabet)
+ Firstborn + and Most New +
Almighty (Greek) + and Ysus + I
Am Who Is + Lamb + Egg + Bull
Calf + Serpent + Ram + Lion +
Worm[83] + One Father + One Son
+ One Holy Spirit + My God, my
God, why hast thou forsaken me?
(Aramaic. Words spoken by Jesus
on the cross) + Jasper brought
gold + Thus Melchior, Antropa,
myrrh + Whoever then carries
the names of these kings with him
+ will be free from the falling sick-
ness by the mercy of the Lord.[84]
+ Ananizapta + Ananizapta +
Ananizapta + Jesus the Nazarene,

---

83. Many of the names derive
from a portion of the Catholic liturgy
known as the "Alma chorus domini."
See Dickinson, *Missale ad usum
insignis*, 1:439–40 ("Feria quinta post
Pentacosten").

84. The scribe or a previous scribe
has incorporated a Latin charm for
epilepsy into this list of divine names,
seemingly unaware of the meaning.

Andreas + Jacobus + Philippus + Simon + Barnabas + Thomas + Iohannes + Tadeus + Marcus Matheus + Lucas + Johannes + vt me defendant ab omni malo et periculo et ab omnibus infirmitatibus meis amen.

3 pr nr 3 avi i c et dicas. In principio erat verbum etc.

Translation/

King of the Jews, Son of God have mercy upon me. Amen. + Heal me and save me and care for me, Lord my God, from every evil and from all of my infirmities. Amen. + Michael + Gabriel + Raphael + Saraphiel + Sariel + Vriel + Tobiel + Barathiel + Reguel + God of Abraham + God of Isaac + God of Jacob + Peter + Paul + Andreas + Jacob + Philip + Simon + Barnabas + Thomas + John + Thaddeus + Mark + Matthew + Luke + John + that they defend from every evil and danger, and from all of my infirmities. Amen.[85]

Say three Our Fathers, three Hail Marys, one Creed, *and say "In the beginning was the word . . . , etc."*[86]

5.11. SPOILING WITCHCRAFT AND THEFT[87]

To spoil a thief or witch or any other enemy and to be delivered from the evil.

Before sunrise.[88] "I gather thee bough of this summer's growth[89] in the name of such a one .N." When you have gathered the wand then cover the table and say "In nomine patris + et filii + et spiritus sancti

85. The Latin is a sentence fragment. It is possible, however, that a main verb such as "I invoke" was understood prior to the list of saints' and angels' names.

86. One is to recite the first chapter of the Gospel of John, a passage commonly used in exorcisms and ritual magic.

87. Oxford, Bodleian Library, e Mus. 173, fol. 37.

88. *Ante solis ortum*

89. Wands were often supposed to be of hazel and made from a sprig of a single year's growth. See, for example, London, British Library, Sloane 3805, fol. 70v.

+ Amen"[90] thrice. And so, striking upon the carpet say as followeth.
"Droche. Myroche. Esenaroth + Betu + Baroch + Ass[91] + maaroth
+." And then say, "Holy Trinity, punish him that hath wrought this
mischief and take it away by thy great justice. Eson + Elyon + Emaris
+ Ales + Age +" and strike the carpet with the wand.

To make a witch confess her evil before you
Take a lambskin made into[92] parchment and make therein two images,
one of a man and another of a woman, and make them on the Saturday
morning at the sun rising and use them in this manner. Take a bodkin
or a nail and look in what place you would have them hurt. In that
place prick them and do so twice or thrice a day and the party that
you shall use so shall never take rest nor sleep until she hath seen you
and required pardon at your hands.

In pricking say as hereafter followeth.

"I compel and constrain thee thou wicked person or you wicked
persons which have committed and done this wicked and devilish act,
by the true God, by the living God, and by the holy God that thou nor
you have no power to withstand or resist any calling but with all haste
and speed possible without delay or tarrying you come unto me and
confess thy naughty and wicked deeds which you hast done. In the
name of God. And also I conjure and constrain thee to come by all
the holy names of God and especially by these: Semurhamephoras[93]
+ Agla + Adonay + Anabona + Panton + Craton + Agyos + Eskyros
+ Athanatos + Messyas + Sother + Alpha + et Omega + Emanuel
+ Sabaoth + Unigenitus + Via + Vita + Homo + Usyon + Principia
+ Cormogenitus + Sapentia + Consolator + Adiuvator + Primus et
Novissimus + El + Elemay + on + Tetragrammaton + and by the holy
name Jesus at which name all things both in heaven in earth and also in
hell do bow,[94] and by the Holy Virgin Mary, mother of our Lord Jesus
Christ, and by St. John Baptist which was the forerunner of our Lord
Jesus Christ, & by the golden girdle which Saint John saw girt about

---

90. = In the name of the Father
and of the Son and of the Holy Spirit.
Amen.

91. Poss. *As8*, a mistranscription of
"alpha and omega."

92. *in*

93. I.e., Shemhemphoras.

94. Philippians 2:10.

the loins of our Lord,[95] and by the two-edged sword that [fol. 37v] proceeded out of the mouth of God,[96] and by all that God is able to do, and by all the powers in heaven, in earth, and under the earth, I adjure you by the seven planets and twelve signs, and by all that you be subject unto, and by all the names of angels, and especially of these, Michael + Gabriel + Raphael + Basquiel + Samael + Anael + Capael + Carafax + Wiel + and by all things that God hath made to the honor and glory of his name that thou or you which have done this wicked and devilish deed have no power to resist nor withstand my calling, but without all delay or tarrying to come speedily in all haste possible in pain or under pain of eternal damnation from worse pain to worse. In the name of the Father, the Son, and the Holy Ghost. Amen."

The experiment of W. Bacon to destroy witches
William Bacon the friar made a bond that all wicked persons should come before him and confess their evil deeds. In the new of the moon, the moon being in airy signs on the Saturday in the hour of Saturn take a piece of parchment and write therein the picture and similitude of the man or of the woman suspected. In his forehead write the name of the person, and on his breast these characters: .♒.♑.♄.[97] And then with a sharp bodkin all to beprick the picture in the head and breast and read this conjuration following:

"I conjure thee or you, .N., witch or witches, by the living God the true God and the holy God, and by all the prophets and patriarchs, martyrs, confessors, and virgins, and by all the holy people which follow the laws of God, and by all angels and archangels, thrones, dominations, principalities, powers, cherubim, and seraphim,[98] and by the four elements, fire, water, air, and earth, and the thirty thunderings and lightnings[99] as sem caph tan sade dalleth, etc. and by the seven planets, Saturn, Jupiter, Mars, Sol, Venus, Mercury, and Luna, and by all the powers pronounced before. I conjure you, witch or witches,

---

95. Revelation 1:13.
96. Revelation 2:16.
97. We assume the scribe knew these were the conventional astrological sigils for Gemini, Capricorn, and Saturn, and have modernized the sigil for Capricorn.
98. *principats, powers, cherubin, and seraphin*
99. The source of this is unclear, possibly Revelation 4:5 or Exodus 20:18.

wheresoever or whatsoever you be, that are within seven miles of this place, no rest to have, but pricking pains, sleeping and waking, until you do come with speed hither into this pool or water, and therein to confess to me some part of your wicked and devilish deeds, which you have done to such a person, .N., by the virtue of the Holy Trinity. Fiat fiat fiat.[100] Amen."

When he or she is come, give them counsel utterly to forsake such wickedness for ever.

100. *Fyat fyat fyat.* = Let it be done. Let it be done. Let it be done.

Conclusion

To understand the practice of magic in Tudor England it is critical to employ the complementary perspectives provided by manuscripts and legal sources. Taken together, these give a more complete view of the practice of magic. We can, for example, understand the magic recorded in manuscripts as socially situated, whether charges of magic reflect the realities of magic practices, the extent to which the ideal practices represented in manuscripts were actually practiced, and the extent to which known practitioners engaged with written traditions.

The points where these two kinds of sources present starkly different pictures also prompt us to ask a range of new and different questions, and to think more subtly about the subject. We find, for example, that certain forms of magic appear frequently in manuscript and very rarely in legal records. In the case of healing magic, it seems clear that there was little motivation beyond moral approbation to accuse anyone of it, and so it rarely found its way into the courts. In the case of "The Eye of Abraham," the high appeal of the text for scribes had less to do with its social and practical feasibility for identifying thieves than with its evocative contents. By contrast, the key-and-psalter method was a compelling popular tradition that was built upon the convincing results it could achieve, and, perhaps due to its popular or nonlearned origins, it was not included in written traditions until quite late.

The comparison of legal and manuscript sources in this volume has led not only to a range of these more specific kinds of observations but also to a number of general arguments about the history of magic in premodern period. Let us highlight a few.

The last chapter includes countermagic against witchcraft. This process was understood by its users to battle the devil and his minions through the power of God. In short, for everyday magicians and their clients, witchcraft was qualitatively different from magic or cunning. This is by no means a novel observation, but it highlights the ways in which the study of witchcraft and of the practice of magic are two halves of a whole. The witch trials were geographically isolated and episodic as well as being far more brutal in their treatment of magic crimes than what was normal. They are thus valuable for revealing the weaknesses of the judicial system or the ways in which communities could engage in pathological behavior. They also highlight cultural predispositions such as misogyny. But the witch trials are a poor gauge for how a society understood and treated magic practitioners and cannot really be understood without reference to these normative conditions and institutional approaches. For that, one needs to look at the sorts of cases and manuscripts we have examined in this book, which were rare but steady. These represent magic that literally was practiced every day, which makes them a critical baseline for understanding the instances of suspected witchcraft and witch trials. It also gives a much more dependable picture of how the premodern societies used, regulated, and understood magic before and after the witch trials, and in all those regions where witch trials never occurred.

One significant area where the records of everyday magic provide an important correction to conventional assumptions lies in the gendering of magic. Magic underwent a "feminizing" process at the start of the fifteenth century in which women were regarded as particularly susceptible to the temptations of magic, and this situation prevailed through to the seventeenth.[1] Such assumptions had their most dramatic expression in the highly misogynistic and ideologically driven witch hunts, but they are also evident in commonly held assumptions. This is despite the fact that everyday magic evidently was performed just as often by men as women in Tudor England, even love and healing magic, traditionally associated with women. This being said, some forms of gendered *preference* are certainly evident, such the preference by men for erotic magic and by women for magic to find or maintain marriages. Our examination of both manuscript and legal evidence provides no simple solutions to these complexities and cultural contradictions. But it makes clear that there are no grounds for

---

1. Bailey, "Feminization of Magic."

assuming that either men or women practiced magic more frequently. It also demonstrates how critical it is to keep all these multiple layers of gendering in mind as one interprets the sources.

Although it was practiced every day, magic was also an uncommon crime. This is to say, it was rare for authorities to prosecute practicing magicians, and the most significant factor that brought them to the attention of the authorities (at least in the cases where this is possible to discern) was social disruption rather than magic in itself. The resulting penalties tended to be corporal punishment and/or public penance and sometimes jail when the magician was in trouble for other reasons such as suspected treason. On balance, authorities had more significant areas of misbehavior to deal with than magic, and so, no matter what they might have said, they tended to focus their energies on other forms of misbehavior. Once again this stands in stark contrast to the more episodic and extreme prosecutions in areas such as Essex. But the disinclination to prosecute magic in more thoroughgoing or draconian ways may also be related to other issues.

We have seen several instances in which authorities refer to magic practitioners as fraudulent or unintelligent, an attitude that may well have been tacitly maintained by others in positions of authority. Thomas Fansome's charming was referred to as unlearned (lewd) and his medical pretensions as false or counterfeit (Text 3.5), and Friar William (Text 2.2) was said to practice theft magic "to the great deceit of the people." There are also cases that clearly appeared in the courts because of the practice of fraud, even if the records explicitly associate *belief* in magic with heresy (e.g. Text 3.3). The identification of magic with fraud was not instantiated in English law until the early eighteenth century and is commonly regarded as an Enlightenment habit of mind. Nonetheless, this evaluation of magic was by no means new among English authorities either religious or secular. This more skeptical (not to mention realistic) attitude may help us understand not only the low numbers of witch trials and executions in England but also the comparatively light treatment of magicians who were presented. It seems quite possible that, although they may have used terms such as "heresy" to refer to the practices, authorities thought of magicians as disruptive petty frauds rather than dangerous enemies of Christendom.

Certainly, one of the reasons for the low number of prosecutions for magic was, as Owen Davies has suggested, the fact that cunning folk were generally regarded with respect by their communities.[2] The evidence presented here largely supports this idea. As the cases in this volume attest, a very significant number of those who appeared in court did so because they failed to retain the respect of their clients, committed some other kind of offense, or played a part in a case not centrally concerned with magic. If manuscripts and anecdotal evidence are any indication, a considerably larger number of practitioners existed than appeared in the courts, and those magicians who did not disrupt the regular functioning of Tudor society generally functioned without interference.

We have also explored another aspect of this situation: the ways in which magic served key roles in a larger social system and was thus seen as positive by most people. It reinforced conventional religious ideas about the power of Christianity and put that power in the hands of individual people. Magic also served as an outlet for anxiety surrounding everyday problems or threats to well-being. Not only did magical practices help people feel as though they had done something proactive, they also did so in a way that was less disruptive to social order than seeking physical revenge, retaliation theft, or acting out in other inappropriate ways. Sometimes they also served to fill certain social vacuums in the control of misbehavior that the legal system did not provide. This is starkly evident in the case of theft magic, where there was a significant range of reasons, both personal and social, for people to employ magical thief identification as a way of getting their goods back or publicly identifying a thief rather than bringing the case to court. This is perhaps the most compelling evidence for understanding why cunning folk were so rarely presented in court. They not only tended to be respected, they played key social roles.

The primary quality of everyday magic is that it seeks to control common problems surrounding love, sex, money, health, social relations, misfortune, and the unknown. Everyday magicians provided the most common magical solutions to those problems. A close look

2. Davies, *Cunning-Folk*, 12, 69, 74–77.

at modern magic reveals little change in the list of problems, and this is no doubt because these issues remain important to us.[3] Although it has been argued that an increased control over nature has driven a decline in magic, the evidence suggests that it has had little effect.[4] In comparison to its premodern progenitors, modern medicine may help us live longer and with greater comfort, and modern science may more accurately describe the causes of misfortune at a physical level, but there remain significant areas in our lives which are utterly beyond our control. And where accepted scientific responses to such misfortunes fail or seem insufficient, we fill in with a plethora of "alternative" approaches not sanctioned by science and rejected as problematic by many contemporary religious groups. It behooves us to consider our own world and our own forms of magic as we seek to understand those of the past. Perhaps the most important lesson to draw from this is that magic and the things for which we use it are very human and very commonplace.

3. See, for example, the operations in Starhawk, *The Spiral Dance: A Rebirth of the Ancient Religion of the Great Goddess* (San Francisco: Harper & Row, 1979), 149–53.

4. This was classically articulated in Keith Vivian Thomas, *Religion and the Decline of Magic* (New York: Scribner, 1971).

APPENDIX:
WORDS OF POWER WITH KNOWN MEANINGS

Word	Meaning	Texts in which it occurs	Occurs in Alma Chorus Domini
Adiuvator	Judge (Latin)	5.11	
Adonay/Adonai	Lord (Hebrew)	2.11, 3.6, 5.7, 5.10, 5.11	*
Athanatos	Immortal (Greek)	5.10, 5.11	*
Agios, Agyos	Sacred (Greek)	1.3, 2.10, 5.11	
Agla	acronym of Hebrew phrase "Thou art mighty forever Lord"	5.7, 2.9,5.10, 5.11	
Agnus	Lamb	4.7, 5.10	*
Alpha et Omega (ω)	first and last letters of the Greek alphabet	2.9, 2.14, 5.10, 5.11	*
Athanatos	Deathless or Immortal (Greek)	2.14	
Consolator	Consoler (Latin)	5.11	
Craton	(ee Panton)	2.11, 2.14	*
Crux	cross (Latin)	1.3	
Dominus	Lord (Latin)	3.6	
El	God (Hebrew)	1.3, 2.14, 5.11	
El/Eli/Ely/Elay/Eloi	God (Hebrew/Aramaic)	2.10, 2.14, 4.7	
Emanuel	God with Us (Hebrew)	2.11, 5.10, 5.11	*
Esykros/Yskyros	Mighty One (Greek)	5.10, 5.11	
Lamazatetham/ lmazabathani	from the phrase spoken by Jesus on the cross, "Eli, Eli, lama sabach-thani" (My God, my God, why has thou forsaken me?) (Hebrew/ Aramaic)	2.14, 5.10	
Messias	Messiah	2.14, 5.10, 5.11	*

Word	Meaning	Texts in which it occurs	Occurs in Alma Chorus Domini
Otheos	God (Greek)	2.14, 5.10	*
Ovis	Egg (Latin)	4.7, 5.10	*
Panton	from Pantocrator, meaning ruler of all or almighty (Greek)	2.10, 2.14, 5.11	*
Primus et Novissimus	First and Most New (Latin)	5.11	
Principia/ Principium	Beginning (Latin)	5.11	*
Rex	King (Latin)	2.11	
Sabaoth	Lord (Hebrew)	2.9, 5.10, 5.11	*
Salvator	Savior (Latin)	2.11, 5.10	
Sanctus	Holy (Latin)	2.11	
Sapientia/Sapiencia	Wisdom (Latin)	5.10, 5.11	*
Sother	Savior (Hebrew)	5.10, 5.11	*
Splendidus/ Splendor	Splendid/Splendor (Latin)	4.7, 5.10	*
Tetragrammaton	the name for the four-letter Hebrew name for God	2.9, 5.7, 5.10, 5.11	
Unigenitus	Only begotten (Latin)	5.10, 5.11	*
Usion/Ysyon	shortened from *homoousion*, which means "same in essence" and refers to the nature of the Trinity (Greek)	5.11	
Via	Way (Latin)	5.11	*
Vita	Life (Latin)	5.11	*

Note: The numerous words in Text 5.10 have not been included in this table since a full translation is provided.

BIBLIOGRAPHY

ARCHIVAL SOURCES

Canterbury
    Cathedral Archives and Library, CC/JQ/307/xiv
Maidstone
    Kent Archives and Local History, DCb/J/Z/3/32
    Kent Archives and Local History, DCb/PRC/44/3
London Metropolitan Archives
    DL/C/B/041/MS09065J/002
    DL/C/B/043/MS09064/003
    DL/C/B/043/MS09064/005
    DL/C/B/043/MS09064/008
    DL/C/B/043/MS09064/010
London, National Archives of the United Kingdom
    TNA C/1/46/425
    TNA C/1/307/41
    TNA PROB/11/40/313
    TNA SP/12/186/188r and 221–25
    TNA SP 226 ff. 119–22
Taunton, Somerset Record Office
    D/D/breg/9 Oliver King
    D/D/ca/1a
York, Borthwick Institute for Archives
    Abp. Reg. 26 Christopher Bainbridge (1509–1514)

MANUSCRIPTS

London, British Library
    Additional 34111
    Harley 424
    Harley 425
    Lansdowne 2/26.

Sloane 3160
Sloane 3542
Sloane 3805
Sloane 3846
Sloane 3849
Sloane 3850
Sloane 3853
London, Wellcome Library
    Wellcome 110
Oxford, Bodleian Library
    Additional B. 1
    e Mus. 173
    e Mus. 238
    Rawlinson D. 252

PUBLISHED SOURCES

"Alma Chorus Domini." In *Analecta hymnica Medii Aevii*, edited by G. M. Dreves and C. Blume, vols. 25 (no. 2) and 53 (no. 87). 55 vols. Leipzig, 1886–1922.

Bailey, Michael D. "The Feminization of Magic and the Emerging Idea of the Female Witch in the Late Middle Ages." *Essays in Medieval Studies* 19 (2002): 120–34.

Bain, Frederika. "The Binding of the Fairies: Four Spells." *Preternature* 1, no. 2 (2012): 323–54.

Bardsley, Sandy. *Venomous Tongues: Speech and Gender in Late Medieval England*. Philadelphia: University of Pennsylvania Press, 2006.

Bayley, John Whitcomb. *The History and Antiquities of the Tower of London, with Memoirs of Royal and Distinguished Persons*. Vol. 2. London: T. Cadell, 1825.

Beattie, J. M. "The Pattern of Crime in England." *Past and Present* 62 (1974): 73–78.

Bellamy, John G. *The Tudor Law of Treason: An Introduction*. Studies in Social History. London: Routledge & Kegan Paul, 1979.

Bennell, John. "Kranich, Burchard [Known as Dr Burcot] (d. 1578), Physician and Mining Entrepreneur." In *Oxford Dictionary of National Biography*. Oxford: Oxford University Press, 2008. https://doi.org/10.1093/ref: odnb/52152.

Bever, Edward Watts Morton. *The Realities of Witchcraft and Popular Magic in Early Modern Europe: Culture, Cognition, and Everyday Life*. New York: Palgrave Macmillan, 2008.

Blanchard, Ian. "Gresham, Sir Richard (c. 1485–1549), Mercer, Merchant Adventurer, and Mayor of London." In *Oxford Dictionary of National Biography*. Oxford: Oxford University Press, 2008. https://doi.org/10 .1093/ref:odnb/11504.

Briggs, K. M. *The Anatomy of Puck: An Examination of Fairy Beliefs Among Shakespeare's Contemporaries and Successors*. London: Routledge & Kegan Paul, 1959.

Briggs, Robin. *Witches and Neighbours: The Social and Cultural Context of European Witchcraft*. London: HarperCollins, 1996.

Callan, Maeve Brigid. *The Templars, the Witch, and the Wild Irish: Vengeance and Heresy in Medieval Ireland*. Ithaca: Cornell University Press, 2015.

Cameron, Alan. "Markham, Sir John (b. Before 1486, d. 1559), Soldier and Member of Parliament." In *Oxford Dictionary of National Biography*. Oxford: Oxford University Press, 2004. https://doi.org/10.1093/ref: odnb/37736.

Chamberlain, Mary. *Old Wives' Tales: The History of Remedies, Charms and Spells*. Stroud, UK: Tempus, 2006.

Church of England, Province of Canterbury, Archbishop (1576–1583: Grindal). *Articles to Be Enquired of, within the Prouince of Canterburie, in the Metropoliticall Visitation of the Most Reuerende Father in God, Edmonde Archbishop of Canterburie*. London: [H. Denham for] Willyam Seres, 1576.

Cockburn, J. S. "The Nature and Incidence of Crime in England, 1559–1625." In *Crime in England, 1550–1800*, edited by J. S. Cockburn, 60–70. Princeton: Princeton University Press, 1977.

Cressy, David. *Birth, Marriage, and Death: Ritual, Religion, and the Life-Cycle in Tudor and Stuart England*. Oxford: Oxford University Press, 1997.

———. *Dangerous Talk: Scandalous, Seditious, and Treasonable Speech in Pre-modern England*. Oxford: Oxford University Press, 2010.

Davies, Owen. *Cunning-Folk: Popular Magic in English History*. London: Hambledon & London, 2003.

Devine, Michael. "John Prestall: A Complex Relationship with the Elizabethan Regime." MA thesis, Victoria University of Wellington, 2010.

Dickinson, Francis Henry. *Missale ad usum insignis et præclaræ ecclesiæ Sarum*. 4 vols. Burntisland: E prelo de Pitsligo, 1861–83.

Dobin, Howard. *Merlin's Disciples: Prophecy, Poetry, and Power in Renaissance England*. Stanford: Stanford University Press, 1990.

Duffy, Eamon. *The Stripping of the Altars: Traditional Religion in England, 1400–1580*. 2nd ed. New Haven: Yale University Press, 2005.

Durston, Gregory. *Crime and Justice in Early Modern England: 1500–1750*. Chichester, UK: Barry Rose Law, 2004.

Eamon, William. *Science and the Secrets of Nature: Books of Secrets in Medieval and Early Modern Culture*. Princeton: Princeton University Press, 1994.

Edsall, Mary Agnes. "*Arma Christi* Rolls or Textual Amulets?: The Narrow Roll Format Manuscripts of 'O Vernicle.'" *Magic, Ritual, and Witchcraft* 9, no. 2 (2014): 178–209.

England and Wales, Sovereign (1509–1547: Henry VIII). *Articles to Be Enquyred of, in the Kynges Maiesties Visitacion.* [London?]: Richardus Grafton regis impressor excudebat, [1547?].

Evenden Nagy, Doreen. *Popular Medicine in Seventeenth-Century England.* Bowling Green: Bowling Green State University Popular Press, 1988.

Ewen, C. L'Estrange. *Witch Hunting and Witch Trials: The Indictments for Witchcraft from the Records of 1373 Assizes Held for the Home Circuit, A.D. 1559–1736.* London: Kegan Paul, Trench, Trubner, 1929.

Fanger, Claire. "Virgin Territory: Purity and Divine Knowledge in Late Medieval Catoptromantic Texts." *Aries* 5, no. 2 (2005): 200–25.

Faraone, Christopher A. *Ancient Greek Love Magic.* Cambridge, MA: Harvard University Press, 1999.

Freeman, Jessica. "Sorcery at Court and Manor: Margery Jourdemayne, the Witch of Eye Next Westminster." *Journal of Medieval History* 30, no. 4 (2004): 343–57.

French, John. *The Art of Distillation, or, a Treatise of the Choicest Spagiricall Preparations Performed by Way of Distillation Together with the Description of the Chiefest Furnaces & Vessels Used by Ancient and Moderne Chymists.* London: Printed by E. Cotes, for Thomas Williams, 1653.

Frere, W. H. *The Use of Sarum.* 2 vols. Cambridge: Cambridge University Press, 1898.

Gaskill, Malcolm. *Witchfinders: A Seventeenth-Century English Tragedy.* Cambridge, MA: Harvard University Press, 2005.

Gentilcore, David. *From Bishop to Witch: The System of the Sacred in Early Modern Terra D'otranto.* Manchester: Manchester University Press, 1992.

Hadass, Ofer. *Medicine, Religion, and Magic in Early Stuart England: Richard Napier's Medical Practice.* Magic in History. University Park: Penn State University Press, 2019.

Hair, P. E. H. *Before the Bawdy Court; Selections from Church Court and Other Records Relating to the Correction of Moral Offences in England, Scotland, and New England, 1300–1800.* New York: Barnes and Noble Books, 1972.

Hale, William, ed. *A Series of Precedents and Proceedings in Criminal Causes Extending from the Year 1475 to 1640: Extracted from Act-Books of Ecclesiastical Courts in the Diocese of London.* London: F. & J. Rivington, 1847.

Hanawalt, Barbara. "Men's Games, King's Deer: Poaching in Medieval England." *Journal of Medieval and Renaissance Studies* 12, no. 2 (1988): 175–93.

Harkness, Deborah E. *John Dee's Conversations with Angels: Cabala, Alchemy, and the End of Nature.* Cambridge: Cambridge University Press, 1999.

Harrison, Brian A. *The Tower of London Prisoner Book.* Leeds: Royal Armouries, 2004.

Harriss, G. L. "Eleanor [née Eleanor Cobham], Duchess of Gloucester (c. 1400–1452), Alleged Sorcerer." In *Oxford Dictionary of National Biography*. Oxford: Oxford University Press, 2008. https://doi.org/10.1093/ref:odnb/5742.

Hawkyard, Alasdair. "Poyntz, Sir Robert (B. Late 1440s, D. 1520)." In *Oxford Dictionary of National Biography*. Oxford: Oxford University Press, 2015. https://doi.org/10.1093/ref:odnb/70796.

Hedegård, Gösta, ed. *Liber Iuratus Honorii—A Critical Edition of the Latin Version of the Sworn Book of Honorius*. Stockholm: Almqvist & Wiksell International, 2002.

Herrup, Cynthia B. *The Common Peace: Participation and the Criminal Law in Seventeenth-Century England*. Cambridge Studies in Early Modern British History. Cambridge: Cambridge University Press, 1987.

Hoak, Dale. "Godsalve, Sir John (b. in or Before 1505, d. 1556)." In *Oxford Dictionary of National Biography*. Oxford: Oxford University Press, 2004.

Hoggard, Brian. "Witch Bottles: Their Contents, Contexts and Uses." In *Physical Evidence for Ritual Acts, Sorcery and Witchcraft in Christian Britain: A Feeling for Magic*, edited by Ronald Hutton. Basingstoke, UK: Palgrave Macmillan, 2016.

Houlbrooke, Ralph A. *Church Courts and the People During the English Reformation, 1520–1570*. Oxford Historical Monographs. Oxford: Oxford University Press, 1979.

Hunt, Tony. *Popular Medicine in Thirteenth-Century England: Introduction and Texts*. Cambridge: D. S. Brewer, 1990.

Ingram, Martin. *Church Courts, Sex, and Marriage in England, 1570–1640*. Past and Present Publications. Cambridge: Cambridge University Press, 1987.

Jansen, Sharon L. *Political Protest and Prophecy Under Henry VIII*. Woodbridge, UK: Boydell Press, 1991.

Jones, Claire. "Formula and Formulation: 'Efficacy Phrases.'" *Neuphilologische Mittelungen* 99, no. 2 (1998): 199–209.

Jones, Karen. *Gender and Petty Crime in Late Medieval England: The Local Courts in Kent, 1460–1560*. Woodbridge, UK: Boydell, 2006.

Jones, Karen, and Michael Zell. "'The Divels Speciall Instruments': Women and Witchcraft Before the 'Great Witch-Hunt.'" *Social History* 30, no. 1 (2005): 45–63.

Jones, Philip E., ed. *Calendar of Plea and Memoranda Rolls, 1458–1482*. Cambridge: Cambridge University Press, 1961.

Jordan, W. K., ed. *Chronicle and Political Papers*. Ithaca: Cornell University Press, 1966.

Kassell, Lauren. *Medicine and Magic in Elizabethan London: Simon Forman, Astrologer, Alchemist, and Physician*. Oxford Historical Monographs. Oxford: Clarendon Press, 2005.

Kavey, Allison. *Books of Secrets: Natural Philosophy in England, 1550–1600*. Urbana: University of Illinois Press, 2007.

Kelly, H. A. "English Kings and the Fear of Sorcery." *Mediaeval Studies* 39 (1977): 206–38.

Kesselring, K. J. "Felony Forfeiture and the Profits of Crime in Early Modern England." *Historical Journal* 53 (2010): 271–88.

———. "Felony Forfeiture in England, c.1170–870." *Journal of Legal History* 30, no. 3 (2009): 201–26.

Kieckhefer, Richard. "Erotic Magic in Medieval Europe." In *Sex in the Middle Ages: A Book of Essays*, edited by Joyce E. Salisbury, 30–55. New York: Garland, 1991.

———. *Magic in the Middle Ages*. Cambridge Medieval Textbooks. Cambridge: Cambridge University Press, 1989.

King, John N. "Underhill, Edward (b. 1512, d. in or After 1576)." In *Oxford Dictionary of National Biography*. Oxford: Oxford University Press, 2010. https://doi.org/10.1093/ref:odnb/27997.

Kittredge, George Lyman. *Witchcraft in Old and New England*. New York: Russell & Russell, 1956.

Klaassen, Frank. *Making Magic in Elizabethan England*. University Park: Penn State University Press, 2019.

———. "Three Magic Rituals to Spoil Witches." *Opuscula* 1 (2011): 1–10.

Klaassen, Frank, and Katrina Bens. "Achieving Invisibility and Having Sex with Spirits: Six Operations from an English Magic Collection, ca. 1600." *Opuscula* 3, no. 1 (2013): 1–14.

Klaassen, Frank, and Sharon Wright. *The Magic of Rogues: Necromancy and Authority in Early Tudor England*. University Park: Penn State University Press, 2021.

Lippe, Robert, and H. A. Wilson. *Missale Romanum Mediolani, 1474*. Henry Bradshaw Society 17, 33. 2 vols. London: [Printed for the Society by Harrison and Sons], 1899–1907.

Loengard, Janet S. "'Plate, Good Stuff, and Household Things': Husbands, Wives, and Chattels in England at the End of the Middle Ages." In *Tant D'emprises = So Many Undertakings: Essays in Honour of Anne F. Sutton*, edited by Livia Visser-Fuchs, 328–40. [Upminster, Essex]: Richard III Society, 2003.

———. "'Which May Be Said to Be Her Own': Widows and Goods in Late-Medieval England." In *Medieval Domesticity: Home, Housing and Household in Medieval England*, edited by Maryanne Kowaleski and P. J. P. Goldberg, 162–76. Cambridge: Cambridge University Press, 2008.

Luhrmann, T. M. *When God Talks Back: Understanding the American Evangelical Relationship with God*. New York: Alfred A. Knopf, 2012.

MacCulloch, D. "Kett's Rebellion in Context." *Past and Present* 84 (1979): 36–59.

Macfarlane, Alan. *Witchcraft in Tudor and Stuart England: A Regional and Comparative Study*. London: Routledge & Kegan Paul, 1970.

Macfarlane, Alan, and J. A. Sharpe. *Witchcraft in Tudor and Stuart England: A Regional and Comparative Study*. 2nd ed. London: Routledge, 1999.

Maxwell-Lyte, Henry, ed. *The Registers of Oliver King, Bishop of Bath and Wells, 1496–1503, and Hadrian de Castello, Bishop of Bath and Wells, 1503–1518*, Somerset Record Society 54. [Frome, UK]: Butler & Tanner, 1939.

Maxwell-Stuart, P. G. *The British Witch: The Biography*. Stroud, UK: Amberley, 2014.

McMullan, John L. *The Canting Crew: London's Criminal Underworld, 1550–1700*. New Brunswick: Rutgers University Press, 1984.

Midelfort, H. C. Erik. "Witch Craze? Beyond the Legends of Panic." *Magic, Ritual, and Witchcraft* 6 (2011): 11–33.

Mitchell, Laura Theresa. "Cultural Uses of Magic in Fifteenth-Century England." PhD thesis, University of Toronto, 2011.

Neal, Derek. "Suits Make the Man: Masculinity in Two English Law Courts, c. 1500." *Canadian Journal of History* 37 (April 2002): 1–22.

Nichols, John Gough. *Narratives of the Days of the Reformation*. London: Camden Society, 1859.

North, Jonathan, ed. *England's Boy King: The Diary of Edward VI, 1547–1553*. Welwyn Garden City: Ravenhall, 2005.

Olsan, Lea. "Charms and Prayers in Medieval Medical Theory and Practice." *Social History of Medicine* 16 (2003): 343–66.

———. "The Corpus of Charms in the Middle English Leechcraft Remedy Books." In *Charms, Charmers and Charming: International Research on Verbal Magic*, edited by Jonathan Roper, 214–37. New York: Palgrave Macmillan, 2009.

———. "The Language of Charms in a Middle English Recipe Collection." *ANQ* 18 (2005): 29–35.

———. "Latin Charms of Medieval England: Verbal Healing in a Christian Oral Tradition." *Oral Tradition* 7 (1992): 116–42.

———. "The Three Good Brothers Charm: Some Historical Points." *Incantatio* 1 (2011): 48–78.

O'Neil, Mary. "Magical Healing, Love Magic and the Inquisition in Late Sixteenth-Century Modena." In *Inquisition and Society in Early Modern Europe*, edited and translated by Stephen Haliczer, 88–114. London: Croom Helm, 1987.

Ormrod, W. Mark. "The Trials of Alice Perrers." *Speculum* 83, no. 2 (2008): 366–96.

Park, Katharine. "Medicine and Magic: The Healing Arts." In *Gender and Society in Renaissance Italy*, edited by Judith C. Brown and Robert C. Davis, 129–49. Georgetown, ON: Routledge, Chapman & Hall, 2016.

Parry, G. J. R. *The Arch-Conjuror of England: John Dee*. New Haven: Yale University Press, 2011.

Pearson, Jo. "Writing Witchcraft: The Historians' History, the Practitioner's Past." In *Palgrave Advances in Witchcraft Historiography*, edited by

Jonathan Barry and Owen Davies, 225–41. New York: Palgrave Macmillan, 2007.

Pelling, Margaret. "Thoroughly Resented? Older Women and the Medical Role in Early Modern London." In *Women, Science and Medicine, 1500–1700: Mothers and Sisters of the Royal Society*, edited by Lynette Hunter and Sarah Hutton, 63–88. Stroud, UK: Sutton, 1997.

Pelling, Margaret, and Frances White. *Medical Conflicts in Early Modern London: Patronage, Physicians, and Irregular Practitioners, 1550–1640*. Oxford Studies in Social History. Oxford: Oxford University Press, 2003.

Poos, Lawrence R. *Lower Ecclesiastical Jurisdiction in Late-Medieval England: The Courts of the Dean and Chapter of Lincoln, 1336–1349, and the Deanery of Wisbech, 1485–1484*. Oxford: Oxford University Press, 2001.

Porreca, David. "Divine Names: A Cross-Cultural Comparison (Papyri Graecae Magicae, Picatrix, Munich Handbook)." *Magic, Ritual, and Witchcraft* 5, no. 1 (2010): 19–29.

Porter, Roy. *Quacks: Fakers and Charlatans in English Medicine*. Stroud, UK: Tempus, 2000.

Procter, Francis, and Christopher Wordsworth. *Breviarium ad usum insignis ecclesiae Sarum*. 3 vols. Cambridge: Alma Mater Academia, 1879–86.

Raine, James, ed. *Depositions and Other Ecclesiastical Proceedings from the Courts of Durham*. Surtees Society 21. London: J. B. Nichols and Son, 1845.

Reformatio Legum Ecclesiasticarum, Ex Authoritate Primum Regis Henrici. 8. Inchoata: Deinde Per Regem Edouardum 6. London, 1641.

Rider, Catherine. *Magic and Impotence in the Middle Ages*. Oxford: Oxford University Press, 2006.

———. *Magic and Religion in Medieval England*. London: Reaktion, 2012.

———. "Women, Men, and Love Magic in Late Medieval English Pastoral Manuals." *Magic, Ritual, and Witchcraft* 7, no. 2 (2012): 190–211.

Riley, Henry Thomas, ed. *Memorials of London and London Life in the XIIIth, XIVth and XVth Centuries*. [S.l.]: Longmans, Green, 1868.

Robbins, Kevin C. "Magical Emasculation, Popular Anticlericalism, and the Limits of the Reformation in Western France Circa 1590." *Journal of Social History* 31 (1997): 61–83.

Roberts, Gareth, and Fenny Smith, eds. *Robert Recorde: The Life and Times of a Tudor Mathematician*. Cardiff: University of Wales Press, 2012.

Rowse, A. L. *Sex and Society in Shakespeare's Age: Simon Forman the Astrologer*. New York: Scribner, 1974.

Ryrie, Alec. *The Sorcerer's Tale: Faith and Fraud in Tudor England*. Oxford: Oxford University Press, 2008.

Scot, Reginald. *The Discouerie of Witchcraft*. London: W. Brome, 1584.

Shagan, Ethan H. "Protector Somerset and the 1549 Rebellions: New Sources and New Perspectives." *English Historical Review* 114 (1999): 34–63.

———. "Rumours and Popular Politics in the Reign of Henry VIII." In *The Politics of the Excluded, c. 1500–1850*, edited by Tim Harris, 30–66. Basingstoke, UK: Palgrave, 2001.

Sharp, W., and L. E. Whatmore, eds. *Archdeacon Harpsfield's Visitation, 1557.* London: Whitehead, 1950.

Sharpe, James. *Crime in Seventeenth-Century England: A County Study.* Past and Present Publications. 2nd ed. London: Longman, 1999.

———. *Witchcraft in Early Modern England.* Harlow, UK: Longman, 2001.

Shorrocks, Derek Martyn Marsh. *Bishop Still's Visitation 1594: And the "Smale Booke" of the Clerk of the Peace for Somerset, 1593–5.* Taunton, UK: Somerset Record Society, 1998.

Singman, Jeffrey L. *Daily Life in Elizabethan England.* Greenwood Press "Daily Life Through History" Series. Westport, CT: Greenwood Press, 1995.

Skemer, Don C. *Binding Words: Textual Amulets in the Middle Ages.* University Park: Penn State University Press, 2006.

Souza, Laura de Mello e. *The Devil and the Land of the Holy Cross: Witchcraft, Slavery, and Popular Religion in Colonial Brazil.* Translated by Diane Grosklaus Whitty. Austin: University of Texas Press, 2003.

Starhawk. *The Spiral Dance: A Rebirth of the Ancient Religion of the Great Goddess.* San Francisco: Harper & Row, 1979.

Thomas, Keith Vivian. *Religion and the Decline of Magic.* New York: Scribner, 1971.

Thompson, A. Hamilton, ed. *Visitations in the Dioceses of Lincoln, 1517–1531.* Vol. 2. Hereford: Lincolnshire Record Society, 1944.

Thompson, E. M., ed. *Chronicon Angliae.* London: Longman, 1874.

Thorndike, Lynn. *A History of Magic and Experimental Science.* 8 vols. New York: Macmillan, 1923–50.

Usher, Roland Greene. *The Rise and Fall of the High Commission.* Oxford: Clarendon Press, 1913.

Veenstra, Jan R. "The Holy Almandal." In *The Metamorphosis of Magic*, edited by Jan N. Bremmer and Jan R. Veenstra, 189–229. Leuven: Peeters, 2006.

Véronèse, Julien. "God's Names and Their Uses in the Books of Magic Attributed to King Solomon." *Magic, Ritual, and Witchcraft* 5, no. 1 (2010): 30–50.

Walker, Garthine. *Crime, Gender and Social Order in Early Modern England.* Cambridge Studies in Early Modern British History. Cambridge: Cambridge University Press, 2003.

Watkin, Aelred, ed. *Dean Cosyn and Wells Cathedral Miscellanea.* Somerset Record Society 56. Frome, UK: Somerset Record Society, 1941.

Wilcox, Judith, and John M. Riddle. "Qusta Ibn Luqa's *Physical Ligatures* and the Recognition of the Placebo Effect." *Medieval Encounters* 1, no. 1 (1995) 1995): 1–50.

Williams, J. F., ed. *Diocese of Norwich, Bishop Redman's Visitation, 1597: Presentments in the Archdeaconries of Norwich, Norfolk, and Suffolk.* Norfolk Record Society 18. [Norfolk]: Norfolk Record Society, 1946.

Woolley, Benjamin. *The Queen's Conjurer: The Science and Magic of Dr. John Dee, Adviser to Queen Elizabeth I.* New York: Henry Holt, 2001.

Young, Francis. *Magic as a Political Crime in Early Modern England.* London: Taurus, 2018.

INDEX

London, National Archives of the
United Kingdom, NA SP 226,
89–97
London, National Archives
of the United Kingdom,
TNAC/1/46/425, 44–45
London, National Archives
of the United Kingdom,
TNAC/1/307/41, 40n9, 42n14
Love, Katherine, 108–9, 111–12
love magic, 61, 66–67
associated with marriages, 67
and canon law, 62
criminal prosecution of, 65, 67–68
as destabilizing influence, 65
and ecclesiastical authorities, 67
and men, 63–65
and Robert Allen, 63, 66
texts on, 75–83
ties with gambling magic, 85
and women, 59–64

Mabley, Robert, 97
Macfarlane, Alan, 10, 105, 108
magic, 110
and canon law, 7
as destabilizing influence, 65, 131
ecclesiastical authorities on, 7–8
ecclesiastical punishments for, 8
and fraud, 131
and gender, 2, 130
legal status of, 10
and murder, 87, 94–95, 108–9
perceptions of, 109
social roles of, 2, 132
See also divination
magic squares, 99
magical practice
and religious items/prayers, 5, 7,
14–15, 40–42, 47, 50–51, 53–58,
75, 81, 105–6, 110, 114, 132
social aspects of, 132
vs. maleficium, 9
vs. witchcraft, 108
magicians

and laws against magic use, 10–11,
26, 30
as street peddlers, 2
vs. witches, 3, 108, 130
See also cunning folk
malefic magic, 5, 9
in Essex, 9
and gender, 12
and Katherine Love, 111
and manuscripts, 13
manuscripts, 13–17, 110
belonging to Robert Allen, 26–27
as entertainment, 59, 64
and gambling magic, 88
and gender, 62–65
on healing, 105, 107–8
and hunting/fishing magic, 85
and love magic, 61, 63–65
and malefic magic, 13
protective charms/healing, 116–27
on thief identification, 40
trade in, 27
vs. court records, 2
writers of, 61
Markham, John, 25–26, 30–31
marriages
and love magic, 67
and women, 60
Mauss, Marcel, 109
medicine
combined with magic, 103–4
false practice of, 72–74
recent scholarship on, 103–4
medieval/early modern legal systems, 6
medieval literature
and Arabic texts, 14–15
and astrology, 15
compared to ritual magic, 15
roots of, 14
medieval medicine, 5
Medieval necromantic texts, 14
medieval science, 5
Menville, 90, 93–94, 96
Midelfort, Eric, 3